ANCIENT IDEALS

IN

MODERN LIFE

ANCIENT IDEALS

IN

MODERN LIFE

FOUR LECTURES DELIVERED AT THE TWENTY-FIFTH ANNIVERSARY MEETING OF THE THEOSOPHICAL SOCIETY, AT BENARES, DECEMBER, 1900.

ANNIE BESANT

GYAN

Published by

GYAN

Gyan Publishing House
5, Ansari Road
Daryaganj, New Delhi-110002
Phone: 011-47034999, 9811692060
E-mail: books@gyanbooks.com

Distribution Network
gyanbooks.com
India, USA, Canada, UK, Australia, France

ISBN: 978-81-212-8967-2 (PB)
First Published, 1901

2nd Impression 2023

Printed at: Gyan Press, Delhi.

ANCIENT IDEALS *IN* MODERN LIFE
AUTHOR: ANNIE BESANT

ANCIENT IDEALS IN MODERN LIFE

ANCIENT IDEALS

IN

MODERN LIFE

FOUR LECTURES DELIVERED AT THE TWENTY-FIFTH ANNIVERSARY MEETING OF THE THEOSOPHICAL SOCIETY, AT BENARES, DECEMBER, 1900.

BY

ANNIE BESANT

Theosophical Publishing Society
London and Benares

1901

CONTENTS.

FOREWORD.

In the following lectures I have endeavoured to discharge the duty incumbent on the spiritual Teacher—however humble the grade—of holding up the ideal to be aimed at, of reproving the evils of the day, of indicating the path along which the ideal may be approached. The task is one beset with difficulties, but not for that reason may it be avoided; cowards shrink back, appalled by obstacles; heroes overcome them.

At the dawning of the twentieth century, India stands near the parting of the ways; one way leads downwards to death, the other upwards to life. Many of her noblest children are hopeless of her future, and would let her expire peacefully rather than prolong the death-passage by remedies deemed useless. Others, loving her well but ignorantly, would, in the effort to save her, cast aside to the winds all her traditions, and seek by modern western medicines her cure—but really her death. Others, yet again, believe that before her there dawns a new era of spiritual life and of material greatness, and would seek to revive her ancient ideals and wed to them all that is best in modern life. Of these am I, who have spoken these discourses, as a first contribution to that end. For I am a humble servant of the great Masters who declared that they would welcome any who would aid them in the task of regenerating India, and I would fain have humble share in that mighty endeavour.

Hitherto in my lectures, during seven years, I have been content to raise the old ideals before the eyes of India and of the world, and to seek to inspire the Hindus with love and reverence for their ancient faith. The work has not been unfruitful. The impulse given to Hinduism by the teaching of H. P. Blavatsky and the work of Colonel H. S. Olcott has been strengthened, and the part played by the Theosophical Society in the revival of Hinduism is admitted by friends and foes alike. But I have observed with regret, though without surprise, that evil has trodden close on the heels of good, and that while religion has been vivified, abuses and superstitions have also shown more vitality. Hence the duty becomes incumbent on me to speak as plainly against these abuses and superstitions, as in favour of the ancient faith. I may not let them be confounded with the Truth I teach, nor may I stand as endorsing them because reproclaiming the immemorial Dharma.

If they triumph, or remain welded into the fabric of Hinduism, India will perish, and perish shamefully. To separate the rotting from the pure is the condition of life, and those love not India wisely who would leave the rotten, veiling it from public gaze, because attached to that which is pure. Corruption spreads, and its spread is death, whether in the body of the individual or in that of the nation. Hence I have spoken plainly of the abuses, and of the need for their extirpation.

A few points, on which I had intended to touch but which were omitted for lack of time, have been added to the lectures, and are distinguished by enclosure within square brackets.

Though the lectures are addressed to Hindus, many of the matters dealt with, specially in the first and last lectures, are applicable outside Hinduism, and describe ideals that might be incorporated generally in modern life, to its great improvement. And, in any case, the raising of India must interest all who belong to the great Empire of which India forms a part.

May the proposals here made, if wise and good, win the assent and support of India's children, and so prove a step towards her redemption.

ANNIE BESANT.

ANCIENT IDEALS
IN
MODERN LIFE.

FIRST LECTURE.

THE FOUR ÁSHRAMAS.

BROTHERS:

For five and twenty years the Theosophical Society has been at work in the world, carrying out, amid many difficulties and against many obstacles, the great work entrusted to its charge. During these five and twenty years it has been gathering experience, it has been learning its strength and its weakness, it has found out many mistakes, it has corrected many blunders, it has learned the lessons of experience, which will serve it well in the centuries that lie ahead. The ending of the twenty-fifth year of the Society coincides with the ending of the century as marked by the Western calculation, and, as you know, just about the same time there ends one of the smaller cycles reckoned from the Eastern standpoint. So we find ourselves to-day at one of those periods in the world's history at which great changes are initiated, and great impulses given for the forward movement of humanity. It is a time of great opportunities, but also a time of great responsibilities, when choices made are full of great results, when steps taken decide the path along which nations will go for many a year, perhaps for many a century to come.

At this standpoint, then, I ask you with me to look forward as well as backward. I ask you to look forward to that which India may become for the world; I ask you to look forward to that destiny which it is within her power to accomplish, if she takes the right step. I call you to stand for a moment at this meeting of the ways, and see along which way you will elect to tread. The choices that the Gods give to the nations are choices which cannot be avoided, but upon the nature of the choice which answers to the summons from above depends the immediate destiny of the nation, and the part which it will have to play in the near future of the world.

The Society founded by some of the great Ṛishis of India to do certain work in the world is a Society that by its very nature and constitution should be prepared to take a leading part in this choice. If among the Hindus who have come into the Society there is not the courage of initiation and the power to help India at this stage of her destiny, then for the East the Society will largely have failed in its purpose, and its failure in the East will bring about its failure in the West. For as momentous to the Society is the way along which it elects to go, as is momentous for the nation the path along which it decides to tread.

For the last seven years I have been living and working among you, trying to understand, trying to grasp the conditions and the difficulties of the situation, trying to see along which road the redemption for India may possibly be found. Surely during these years I may at least have so lived as to win from you trust enough to believe that my heart is Hindu as yours, my faith and my hope the same as yours; and if in the study that lies before us I speak words with which any of you may disagree—and on such topics disagreement is inevitable—I pray you to believe that I speak with pure intent, with love for India, and for India's faith. Any errors I may make are errors of the head, not of the heart, and if on some points I have to speak on facts that I—and I think most of you—look on with grief and shame, it is in the hope that, recognising the facts, we may find a way to lead India out of her present condition, that we may find the road where the blessings of the Gods may rest on India, leading her to take her right place amid the nations, and fitting her to be the spiritual teacher of mankind.

In speaking of the subjects there is a definite plan that I propose to follow. First, I shall sketch the ancient ideal, so far as I can, of course—for no tongue of man may sketch that divine ideal as it really is in the eyes of the Gods and in the hearts of the great Ṛishis who threw down the reflection of that image on the world. But at least I hope so to speak of that ideal that you may see its beauty, that, above all, you may estimate its value, not only to India, but to the whole world at large. It does not exist for any one land, though it was given to one land; it exists for all the world; but it cannot spread over the world unless it spreads from its centre. The ancient ideals are in your charge, placed in your hands by Those who gave them to the Indian people; and it must not be that, in any change needed to adapt India to modern environment, those great ideals shall be blurred or their brightness diminished. They must keep their full spiritual glory, their fair proportions, and their pure outlines. All changes must be to make them again shine out in practice, and not to alter or lower them according to the passing fashions and fancies of the day.

I shall, in every case, first try to put the ancient ideal before you, and then, in sad and bitter contrast, the present as it is—a contrast so terrible and so heart-breaking that any lover of India might well weep tears of blood over what might be the ideal and what is the actual in India, a contrast so terrible indeed that, were it not that we believe that the Gods are ever watching over India, we might sink down and say that no revival for India is possible. But since we believe that the spiritual forces are mighty enough to subdue all things, there still lingers in the hearts of some of us the hope that India may yet produce children spiritual enough to lead the necessary changes along the right road, with hearts heroic enough to sacrifice themselves for the mother of us all, and so make possible the redemption of which we dream, for which we dare to hope.

The third part of each discourse, then, after the ideal and the actual, will deal with the changes which may lead India from her present position to the height which is her rightful place, and which she ought to occupy in the world of the future, in the evolution of humanity, her rightful place as the teacher, the spiritual teacher, of mankind. This is the study to which we are going to devote ourselves, and to this I shall try to win your assent and sympathy, and more, your active work. The first lecture will be largely of the nature of an introduction, and I fear it may tax your patience by its length, for I want to put before you a world-picture. Unless I can show you the great goal at which we are to aim, all the later proposals will be unintelligible, and will lose their power to attract you by their fitness for the proposed end. You must see the goal, before you can estimate the rightness or the wrongness of the path that assumes to lead to it. And that goal is a greater one than many of you dream.

I must open by asking you to take a wider look at history than you are wont to do, and that not from the standpoint of the physical plane, where nation is warring against nation, where one is jealous of the other, where the desire of one is to rule the other, where there is the hatred of the oppressed and the tyranny of the strong. Leave all these things aside; they are but the things of the physical plane. Let us rise to a point whence some glimpses of the divine plan may be seen, so that we may be able to recognise at least something of the part to be played in connection with it by the nation with which we are concerned.

Where is India standing now? what is her environment? Looking back over the past centuries, we see that nation after nation has invaded India, has tried to settle in her, and has tried to rule her. One nation after another has been, as it were, tried, in order to find out whether it had the qualities in it which made a common future with India possible. See how one nation after another from the West has tried to establish itself within her borders. You need not go so far back as to the invasion of the Greeks, to see how one European nation after another has made a little footing on India's soil, and then has fallen into the background. You only need to look two or three centuries back to see how the Portuguese, the Dutch, the French, have made attempts to dwell on Indian soil, and yet have well-nigh disappeared. Then there came a colony from the far West, the colony of England, and that has grown, has spread, has increased its power, until at the present day we find the great dominant power of England extending directly over the greater portion of India, and influencing very largely those portions of the country which are not under her immediate sway. As a result of this we find here East and West living side by side, England and India established in this vast peninsula—parts, as it were, of one great Empire, an Empire which shows signs of becoming one of the great world-empires of history.

We see as we glance backwards, that from time to time on the stage of history there arises a power which moulds into one nationality many nations, and builds up a mighty fabric of a world-empire, ruling undisputed over the earth. You will find that every sub-race of what the Theosophists call our great Áryan Race has had such a world-empire in connection with its own development. The first branch of the Áryan people who settled to the south of the Himâlayas built a mighty empire. Though the Áryan civilisation was not far extended, and outside the borders of India most of the people were uncivilised, and there existed great masses who were barbarians, still we find them paying tribute and under due subordination, and the great rulers of the earth were along the line of the past monarchs of India. When we follow the birth of one sub-race after another, the same truth comes out. The world-empire of the Accadians, the Babylonian, which joined Babylon and Chaldea, is another world-empire belonging to another sub-race. Then, coming to the sub-race of the Iranians, we have the empire of Persia dominating the civilised world and ruling over the subject nations. Then we find the world-empire of the Keltic sub-race, with its centre in Rome, dominating the world as did the other empires that had passed away before it. Each of these world-empires nursed in itself the growth of its own sub-race, and formed the guard around the cradle in which the new sub-race was born. The fifth sub-race, the Teutonic, has not yet completed itself, and already signs are visible that it has to accomplish this same destiny in human evolution. There is dawning now on the vision of the earth a vast Teutonic world-empire, formed by the English and their Colonies, with their huge offshoot the United States, and with the Germans bound in close alliance. That world-empire will be the next to dominate humanity, in order that, by its power imposing peace upon the world, it may be the cradle of the next sub-race, whose watchword is Peace instead of war, whose watchword is Brotherhood instead of competition. That race will be born in the midst of the world-peace, and peace will be characteristic of its civilisation. What is the part that India is to play therein?

You find her a conquered nation, won by the sword, ruled by the sword, and that sword held in the hand of the dominant factor in the coming world-empire. But at the same time you find her thought, her teaching, her ancient literature, translated into the English tongue—which is the most widely-spread tongue on the earth, and is fast becoming the world-language, which is spreading in every direction, which is talked by the foremost nations of the world. Thus, while politically she is subject, her thought is beginning to dominate the whole of that Western civilisation. That is the first point which marks the place that India will have in this great evolution. In the older days she was the spiritual teacher of the world, and now nations are being prepared to recognise her again in that loftiest and most sacred of characters. Her great teachings are becoming assimilated all over the world through this vehicle of a world-language which is being made part of our own national life. As her teachings are more and more widely accepted, what will be the one supreme teaching which will come as the key-note of the next civilisation?

The great teaching of India, the most precious, the most vital, and the most far-reaching, is the unity of the Self, the one Self in which all things are, and which lives and moves in all. That is India's central and most important teaching. There is one Self, one Existence. In that Life all other lives inhere. In that consciousness all other consciousnesses have their roots. There is but One, without a second, and in That all things exist.

That is the teaching which, spoken by the mouth of India, is spreading over the whole world, and behold! that is the very key-note of the race that is to be born. That race will recognise the spiritual unity of all humanity. Therefore is that unity the one obligatory object of the Theosophical Society, the recognition of the Brotherhood of man, which can only be defended on the ground of a spiritual unity. All men are brothers, no matter what their colour may be, no matter what their race, no matter what their traditions, customs, and origin may be; they all are within the spiritual unity which underlies all mankind. That is the keynote of the next sub-race, the mark of the coming civilisation. Is it without significance that the key-note of the coming sub-race is the supreme teaching of India?

If this possession of the teaching is to bear fruit, what is the next step that India must take? India must fit herself for her great position, and build up a nation worthy to be the spiritual teacher of mankind. If India can do that, if she can build up again her religion in the purity of ancient ideals, in possession of all the spiritual forces contained in the inheritance of the past; if India can train her sons to be noble in character, pure in life, lofty in intelligence, spiritual in aspiration; then India's part in the world-empire will be not the part of a conquered nation, but of an integral part of that empire, honoured as the teacher and religious guide of the nations of the world. She will be no longer a subject nation, but will be a part of a mighty commonwealth, some of her sons sharing the burden of the world-empire as counsellors and rulers, while her teachers bring their great religion to spiritualise every other faith, bring the wisdom of the past to enlighten the ignorance of the present, noble, honoured, and everywhere revered. That is the possibility before you, but only if you rise to the height of your destiny, and fit yourselves to be entrusted with such mighty power.

That, then, is the goal to be aimed at. And the means is the training, the education of the people, the raising of man by man until the whole nation is raised. Do not deceive yourselves by imagining that the greatness of the past will make by itself the greatness of your future. If *you* cannot rise to greatness, there is no greatness possible for India. For the greatness of a nation is measured by the individual greatness of her sons, and unless Indians can be great how can India be mighty? Have you the stuff in you to make part of such a world-empire? Only the Gods can tell. But they have given you the opportunity, which shows that the possibility is there. For the Gods never offer opportunity, unless the one to whom it is offered has in him the possibility of success. It is for us to try to build that success, not only into a possibility, but into a certainty, as may be done if our hearts are heroic, and if we are willing to strive to make ourselves worthy of that future.

Such, then, the goal. The critical question now is: Can India adapt herself to this modern environment? A part of India is determined not to move at all, but to stay where it is. That means death! Life may be measured by the power to adapt the body, the mind, and the whole nature, to the environment in which by the divine Providence an organism is placed. People talk of "the spirit of the age"—some with enthusiasm, some with contempt; some with love, some with hatred; some with a desire to go with it, and some with a desire to oppose it. What is then "the spirit of the age"? Fundamentally, it is the divine impulse carrying man along the road of evolution. It is often surrounded by blunders, often hidden by mistakes, often impeded by the childish ignorance of those whom Íshvara is endeavouring to guide. The true "spirit of the age" should and must be studied, in order that we may see whither the divine Will is leading the world. Do you think that any other will can guide this world, save the Will of Íshvara Himself? Are men so strong, do you imagine, that they can turn the car of evolution against the Will of Íshvara? Amidst the jarring wills, the foolish deeds, the mistakes, the blunders, and the sins of mankind, that one divine Will is working out its unchangeable purpose, and moulding even men's follies and crimes to the working out of its own supreme purpose. For humanity is the potter's clay which is set on the wheel, and as the potter turns his wheel so does Íshvara turn the world-wheel, whereon the clay is human heart and human mind, and the vessels are formed by Him and by none other. We are blind and foolish if we set ourselves against the deep-running tendencies of the day. Many tendencies are superficial, but our duty is to study and to understand the main current, the current of evolution, and then to bring our energies to co-operate with the Divine purpose; for all that goes against that Will must be shattered into pieces, while all that goes with it is part of His life and an organ of His work. To set ourselves stubbornly to stand in one place, and to say: "Because this in the past was good, therefore it must be good for the present and the future, therefore I will not mould myself to the tendencies of the age, nor adapt myself to my environment"—that is to be dead, that is to be fossilised, that is to be left behind in the forward march of evolution. On the other hand, to go forward with headlong precipitancy, without thought or consideration, without reverence for the past, without understanding the causes it has set up, the tendencies it has bequeathed—that spells ruin, as much as immoveability and fossilisation spell death.

Between these two dangers, then, the nation has to steer its way. Between those who will change nothing, so that India cannot live; and those who will change everything, so that India will practically disappear. Neither of these roads is the road that the wise should tread. We should preserve the Indian type, the Indian spirituality—that is the problem. For spirituality is India's special charge in the world's future. But while preserving India's type and India's spirituality, we should weave into India's national life everything good, everything valuable that every other nation has to give, every thing of value that modern progress has acquired; we should choose and discriminate, take what is good and reject what is evil; neither become Westernised by swallowing everything that the West has, without regard to India's type; nor become a dead fossil, interesting to the geologists of the future, bearing no part in the living evolution of the race. This is the problem. If we can solve it rightly, then India has a future, a future so glorious that it will be greater than her past. If we cannot solve it, then India falls out of the nations of the world, and some other nation, taking up her knowledge and welding it with all that is good in the West, will take the place that is India's birthright, as eldest son of the Áryan race. But surely that shall never be her fate! She cannot disappear from the world—India, beloved of the Gods! She cannot thus vanish from the world's history, while They are ruling!

Make no mistake; if this is to be done, it is to be done by sacrifice; for no good thing is won without sacrifice, no great gift is given save when the fire of sacrifice has gone up to heaven and made its appeal to the mighty Ones there. India cannot be redeemed, unless India's sons are ready to give themselves for their race, to offer themselves up on the altar of sacrifice for India's future. For prejudices are strong; there is a mass of ignorant prejudices and conventions against which the bravest hearts must dash themselves, in order to break it down. Some hearts will be broken in the attempt, but as they break they will leave their impress on that wall of dogged prejudice, and it will be the weaker because they have suffered. Are there any among you prepared to act as well as speak, prepared to live as well as talk? Will you give merely what is so easy to give—the applause of your hands, instead of the work of your lives? Will you speak warmly in this hall for the changes that must be made in order that India may live, and then go out into the world outside and live the life of the majority, as though the ideal was never put before you, doing what everybody does? Have you not in you the courage and the devotion to set an example and to give up your own social position, nay, even your lives—or far far harder, your children's lives—to sacrifice those on the altar in order that India may survive? If some of you will do that, then the future is secure. But if you are all cowards at heart, then the sentence will pass, destiny will put its pen through India's name, and India will exist no more.

Such, then, are the introductory ideas that govern these lectures. Let us pass from them to the ideals of the past, to the actual of the present, and to the future that we are going to try to build. [I shall not in this quote many texts, and thus enter into a war with commentators. Texts may be found in support of opposed views, if taken alone, without context and qualification. Persons of most divergent ideas appeal to the same authorities. I shall put the ideal before you, as I have been taught of it, as I have seen it, letting its own beauty and sweet reasonableness recommend it to your hearts and consciences. Here and there I may refer to sacred literature for illustration, but I am not building up these ideals by a laborious comparison of texts, but from a knowledge of the facts.]

The special part of our subject that we are going to study to-day is comparatively easy. No very serious opposition in the minds of many is likely to arise about it. There is one point, however, which will need the sacrifice of which I have just been speaking, in order that it may be practically worked out. But for the most part the road is fairly clear with regard to the four great ideals in life.

A life which is well-ordered from beginning to end—that is what is implied in the phrase, "the Four Áshramas." Two of them—namely that of the student and that of the householder—these two may be said to represent in the life of an individual that outward-going energy which carries the Jîva into what we call the Pravritti Mârga—that great path of action along which the world rolls, and which each individual man treads within the limit of a life in his own little way. The life of the student and the life of the householder, these form the Pravritti Mârga of the individual. The two later stages—the life of the Vanaprastha and that of the Sannyasî—these are the stages of withdrawal from the world, and may be said to represent the Nivritti Mârga in the life of the individual. It is well to recognise this, so as to have an orderly view of life. So wisely did the ancient ones mark out the road along which a man should tread, that any man who takes this plan of life, divided into four stages, will find his outgoing and indrawing energies rightly balanced. First, the student stage, properly lived and worthily carried out; then the householder stage, with all its busy activity in every direction of worldly business; then the gradual withdrawal from activity, the turning inward, the life of comparative seclusion, of prayer and of meditation, of the giving of wise counsel to the younger generation engaged in worldly activities; and then, for some at least, the life of complete renunciation. Any man who takes this plan of life and lives it out will find that he cannot have a life which should be more wisely ordered, which should be made better than that, in which to spend his days from birth to death. This is not an ideal for one nation only, but for all nations, not for one time, but for all times; one half of the life active and stirring, the other half quiet, self-controlled, and self-contained. In the East and in the West alike this ancient ideal of a well-ordered life might well be revived, might well be again practised; and then we should not see on the one hand the pitiable spectacle of boys thrown into the life of the householder before their time has come; and on the other, the equally pitiable spectacle of the old man, whose heart should be turned to the higher life, still grasping money and power, until death wrenches away what he will not voluntarily loose.

Let us take the four stages in order, and consider each. First the student life. What was the ideal of the past? That you may read in detail in your books; here I shall outline it only. The boy was placed in the hands of his teacher to be trained and educated on every side of his nature. The education given to him was one which drew out his powers in the four great factors which form the human constitution. First, we always read of boys that they were versed in the Vedas. The boys were taught religion; they were trained in the sacred literature of their faith, and in the actual daily practice of their religious ceremonies. Thus we find that Râma Chandra was not only thoroughly trained in the knowledge of the Scriptures, but also that He performed His Sandhyâ morning and evening; and was thus trained in the outer religious duties, as well as in sacred learning, both being necessary for the evolution of spirituality. You know how, under the wise hands of His teacher, He learned the great Science of the Self, the Secret of Peace; how His religious nature was trained and developed—He who needed no education save for the instruction that His example might give as to how the young should be trained. That is the first note of ancient education.

The next point is, that the boys were trained in morality. The moral nature was trained as well as the spiritual. They were taught to be obedient, reverent, truthful, brave, courteous, to love and respect their parents and teachers, to be unselfish, to concern themselves with the welfare of those around them. "He was intent on the welfare of others." That is given as the crown of the moral education of the boy.

In the third place, the intellect was trained. The boys were taught the different branches of science and instructed in various kinds of theoretical and practical knowledge. Intelligence, the third part of human nature, received its proper training along with the spiritual and the moral.

Lastly, the body was trained. The physical part received due attention. They were taught games and manly exercises, to ride, to drive, to manage their own bodies, and the bodies of the animals who serve the needs of man.

Thus the education given was all-round education. Every part of man's nature received its proper training. The result was, that when the boys went out into the world, they went out ready to play their parts as members of a great state, as citizens of a great nation—highly pious, moral, learned, and strong. These four great characteristics marked the result of education in ancient India.

What do we find in modern India? An education directed to one part of the boy's nature only, developing the intelligence, training the intellect, but leaving entirely on one side the spiritual nature, and the moral or emotional nature disregarded. The education as now given disregards for the most part the physical nature also, centring itself on the growth of intelligence, on the development of intellect alone. Even that, I may say in passing, is not done in the best possible way.

Such an education as that can never build up a

true man of the world, able to discharge his duties in the world. Only one part of him has been developed, only one quarter of his whole nature has been trained; moral character has been neglected, spirituality has been ignored, body has been left weak, overstrained, overworked. What sort of a nation can you have where the education given to its young is but one quarter of what it should be—one-fourth only given, and that, too, imperfectly and inadequately? What is the result? You get plenty of clever men, but for the most part they are selfish, thinking only of their own aims, each man fighting for his own hand, careless of the welfare of the nation as a whole, gaining for himself or for his family, caring not how others suffer provided that he succeeds, looking on with cold and indifferent eyes at all wrongs perpetrated around him, his heart not moved with sympathy for the trouble and the misery of the people. He is a man developed in intelligence, but lacking in character, in self-respect, in public spirit, in straightforward speaking of truth, in uprightness of words and life. That is the result we see around us, the result of the neglect of religion and of morality. How many men to-day are "intent upon the welfare of others," forgetful of their own success? How many realise that no man can truly succeed, unless he raises others with him at the same time? how many remember that there is only one Life, that the man who tries to wrench himself away from it, in selfishness and indifference, only succeeds in shutting out much of the Life from himself, and that the wall that he builds to exclude his neighbour from himself excludes himself from the Life that flows around him?

What are we then to do—to do practically, and not in theory only, not leaving for the future that work which must be done now? As you know, the attempt to bring back the ancient ideal is already being made in your midst. This very College, in the hall of which I am now speaking, is the work of those who are vowed to the restoration of the ancient type of education, of that four-fold training of the nature which alone can build up the India of the future, though not seeking to reproduce entirely the old models. It is the ideal that we must see, and that we must reproduce in modern garb, adapting it to the times. Would it surprise you to know that in the English nation this four-fold education is even now being given, in the Public Schools and Universities? If you go to any English Public School, you will find that it begins its work every day with the worship of God and the reading of the Christian Scriptures.

Every boy is taught to worship, and is trained in definite moral ideals. You will find that not only is religion thus taught along with morality, but that a good physical training is also given, and insisted upon in the great Public Schools. Every boy is made to play, to exercise his body, to work his limbs, and strengthen his muscles. And if you go to Harrow, Eton, Rugby, or Winchester, you will find the four-fold education there, though of course on Christian lines. The old ideal is being worked out there in principle, and the fundamental ground-plan of the education is right and sound, and it makes patriots as well as all-round developed men. While they nourish love of religion, they nourish patriotism at the same time. If you go to Harrow School Chapel, you will find its walls decorated with brass plates, bearing the names of old Harrow boys who have served their country well. So that when the boys worship God, they see before their eyes the names of the old Harrow boys who once sat where they sit, who as men have given up their lives in times of need for Queen and Country, who have died for Fatherland, and who have held the name of England high among the nations. No boy can worship in that Chapel without receiving some inspiration to heroic living, without welding his love of country into his religion. The boys' ideals are moulded in this way, and they grow up country-loving, patriotic, proud of their land, and so worthy to be citizens of their country. We must revive this education here.

How is this to be done? Is it to be done by forty or fifty people like ourselves, who are weak in number and in intellectual power, if we be left unsupported? No. Do you not realise that this question is *your* question, not ours only? Your boys are the future citizens of India. What are you doing to educate them in the ancient ideals, which will make them worthy citizens? It is not enough to applaud me! Are you working for this education? Are you giving to it your time, your labour, as you would give them to some object which would go to make your own happiness? If you do not do that, what right have you to cheer when other people work, and give mere empty applause?

With regard to this education I have somewhat more to say; and here comes a point for which I ask your careful, your thoughtful, attention. I find, when I read the old Scriptures, that during the period of student life, the student was always under the vow of Brahmacharya. I find every student was under that vow of virginity, of absolute celibacy; and until the student period was over he was not permitted to enter the household life. Thirty-six, eighteen, or nine years—these are the periods given for the student life. During that period absolute celibacy was imposed upon the student. Until that period was over he was not allowed to take a wife, and we often read of a man as a warrior, before he became a husband. What has become of that old ideal in modern India? Boys in school are found to be fathers of children; boys who have not yet even passed into College are found with a baby at home, a child the son of a child. It is utterly against the old ideals. It is destructive of India's life. What is the result? That a boy, at the end of his College life, is often weak in body, his nervous system is weakened, his brain-power is exhausted, and he is a wreck physically when he ought to be in the full flush and vigour of manhood. The pressure of modern education puts a heavy strain upon him, and then, added to that, are the duties of the husband, the responsibility of the father. My brothers, it is not right. It means the ruin of India. You find yourselves old, when you ought to be but of middle age. Do you not see that you are not what you should be? Do you not see that the brain does not and cannot bear the tremendous strain put upon it?

Do you not see that the stature of Indians is growing less? Where the marriages are the earliest, there the stature is the lowest, and it is getting worse and worse. In some parts of India the marrying of a baby in the cradle is permitted, and this is followed by very early parent-hood. Is that a part of India's life, as it was meant to be moulded by the great Gods who gave Their laws through ancient legislators?

This is a question the answer to which is in your own hands. The difficulty we know well enough. For a man who dares to act according to the ancient ideals will find himself surrounded by hundreds of unkind critics, men who have not the courage to act, although in their hearts often longing for and desiring change. How many fathers have told me: "Yes, we know that it is necessary;" but how few have the courage to act upon their opinion, and face the social difficulties that action would bring. Yet only by such courage are great changes made, and nations redeemed. We have come down through cowardice, we must mount through courage. We have become degraded through ignorance, we must rise again by education and restoring the old ideals. If some of you have the courage to say: "We will not act against the ancient rules; we will not do that which we know to be wrong morally and to be evil physically," and if you will therefore make the marriage period later, no matter who may oppose, then you will begin to take the first practical step towards the training of a stronger, manlier, and more vigorous race. I am not asking you to throw off the old customs and to adopt new ones, as some others have advised. I am asking you to restore the old. And I suggest as a step that the first marriage of a girl might be at 14 and of a boy at 18, and the second actual marriage two years later for both. If this rule were followed, you would soon see the effects in the strengthening of the race. I do most earnestly hope that we may begin to set this example gradually in this School and College. We cannot make the full change back to the old ideal at once, but I do trust that we may be able gradually to work towards the ancient ideal, and thus may set an example which all lovers of India will venture to follow, that we may strike the key-note of a better physical future for India, and build up a stronger manhood.*

After the student stage was accomplished, and

* Since these words were spoken, the Managing Committee of the C. H. College has decided to admit no married boys to the Middle Division of the School.

the boy had grown to manhood, then he had to enter upon household life. What influence that household life has upon the evolution of character, you must know if you realise its intention. It is the great school of unselfishness, of temperance, of learning to help the weak, of learning self-sacrifice in the easiest way, where love leads to sacrifice and rewards it as it is made. The love of husband and wife, the purest and noblest of earthly feelings, nearest the love of the soul to God Himself; the love of father for children, of children for father, with the protection given on the one side and the gratitude and veneration given on the other; these are the household educators of the soul. It is said truly that all the other Áshramas take refuge in this, as their strong support. Learning to be detached in the middle of attachment, learning the lesson of chastity where all power of enjoyment is held—these are some of the lessons of family life. But how much change is wanted, if the old beautiful ideal is to shine out clearly. On this I shall have to speak more when I come to deal with India's Womanhood. There is no ideal of marriage like the Indian ideal, only that ideal is rarely found fulfilled to-day.

Consider the father and the children. Is the ideal of that relationship carried out in modern

India? Is not there too much reserve on the one side, and too much timidity on the other? Is not the relationship of father and son too often lacking in frank confidence on the side of the son? Do the fathers think enough of the happiness and amusement of the son, making the home-life bright and attractive? Are they not too often self-centred and indifferent to the wants of the sons, too forgetful of the cravings of youth? The boy is often too shy, alas! to speak to the father, and so the son goes out and finds amusement hand-in-hand with vice, where he ought to have found it with his father's sympathy, and so hand-in-hand with virtue. Indian boys too often go astray because of the want of sympathy and frank friendship with their parents—by the parents laying all stress on authority and little stress on tenderness. Boys need tenderness and sympathy, and loving guidance in the hot days of youth. I say this, because boys sometimes come to me with complaints on their lips that their home life is so dull and dreary that they long to get away from it. Authority is too stringent and too unsympathetic, and hence a tendency in sons to rebel. Where the son shows rebellion, the father is often far more to be blamed than the son. It is the lack of sympathy with the impulses and cravings of youth that often leads to revolt. The father's lack of tenderness and sympathy has as its inevitable result the rebellion of the son, not always expressed, but none the less dangerous. The father ought to be his truest friend, his dearest sympathiser, his most loving counsellor, and where a son finds his father to be such that son is never rebellious. When we find trouble in the home, we must look for its cause to the superior rather than to the inferior. Most breaches in relationship begin in the fault of the higher, and not in that of the lower. When the higher fails in his duty, it is then that the lower begins to fail also.

That is a matter for each man to think out for himself. For the ideal is where the father is his son's best friend, and the son is the father's most loved companion. Let every one see how far this is true in his own home. There is a fatherly love where uttermost tenderness meets folly and transgression, and redeems them by its divine force. If that true household life could be restored, then the active life in the world will be led as it should be, and we shall see everywhere the ancient models of the true grihastha; then will be seen at the end of the household life a readiness to pass on into the next stage, where active life is given up, and the life of religious meditation is carried on.

How shall we adapt the Vanaprastha stage to modern life? It is scarcely in accordance with the modern idea to go into a jungle, to take refuge in a cave, in order to spend in seclusion the later years of life. Modern civilisation trains men in a way which scarcely leaves them fit to take to that actual mode of life, so complex have grown men's wants in modern times. But might it not be possible for the elders amongst us to gradually let go all money-making, to let go all household authority, to let go all business and the taking of an active part in life, letting the younger ones take their places in these respects? Can they not turn to the Nivritti Mârga? Might it not be that they should pass into a life of quiet and dignified partial seclusion, where their lives might be chiefly given to worship, meditation, thought, and development of the higher nature, and where they would always be available as the wisest of counsellors, rich in life's experience, and all the better counsellors because their personal interest had gone in the matters on which they gave counsel, and thus the advice would be free from prejudice and bias. Would not India be the richer if the old men performed that part of their duty, if, withdrawing from activity, they became the guides and advisers of the young, trusted and loved because they had experience and wisdom, and were willing to give them to the young? Would not the re-establishment of that Áshrama be a great blessing in modern life?

The last stage of Sannyâsa needs such high spiritual development that few probably would be able to pass into it. But if that is not now quite possible, it would become possible a few generations hence, when the general level of spirituality had risen under the right living of the three preceding Áshramas.

[As the name of Sannyâsî is common enough in modern India, it may be well to say here that household life is a stage which very few can afford to avoid, so important is it as a spiritual school. Wisely did the Indian Sages prescribe it as of well-nigh universal obligation, for few and far between are those who can lead the life of the true Sannyâsî even in old age, and still fewer are those who can safely embrace it in youth. It is true that there is no fairer ideal than that of the Bâla Yogî, the spotless Kumâra, the boy Saint. When a great Soul incarnates for the helping of the world, he may lead the ascetic life from childhood. But too many lads and young men hastily take the garb of the Sâdhu in modern days, allured by its outer freedom and absence of care and responsibility, adopting it in order to avoid burden, and not in order to bear a heavier one. Robust and lazy, such men swarm over the country by thousands, living on the earnings of others, and giving nothing back in benefit to the community; too often profligate, taking advantage of their sacred garb to corrupt and lead astray, sensualists not ascetics, luxurious not self-controlled. The true Sannyâsî is of priceless value, and the poorest may rejoice to share with him his scanty meal; his spiritual value outweighs a millionfold any physical need he may have; his purity and devotion still purify the atmosphere, and preserve spirituality from perishing outright. But the Sâdhus who are vicious and lazy, useless alike to the Gods and to men, these shame the old ideal and turn men's hearts against the very name of Sannyâsa. For the young men then, except in rare cases, the life of the household, with its compulsory responsibilities and inevitable burdens. Through these a man learns to rule himself, to master his lower nature, and then he can be free without danger to himself and to the community.]

The great ideals of the past, adapted to the present and worked out in modern India, would spread from India to other nations of the world and would gradually mould them into the same rational, wholesome method of living, and thus the whole world would be changed and carried on. We should gradually see in the Western world, as well, the purity of youth, the unselfish, generous life of the householder, replacing the competitive ideals of modern civilisation. We should see old men retiring, and becoming counsellors and guides of families, and a few here and there showing the great ideal of complete renunciation, of utter indifference to all that the world can give. Is it not worth while to rebuild that ideal here, where its roots are still struck, and where men's hearts still cherish it, and thus give to the world a bright object lesson of human life led in a reasonable spiritual fashion, of every part of man developed in its place and used for the good of the community?

That is the thought that I would ask you to take away from this first of our evenings together. Study your own practical daily life, and see where it fails, and when you have seen this, then steadily walk along the road which will bring the ancient ideal back amongst us as a living fact. Do not act impulsively, but carefully think out the question, and when you have thought it out, then act. Do not be content with idle dreaming; do not be content with simple aspiration and pious hope.

Do not say: "We hope that in the future India will go along these lines." But rather say: "By the blessings of the Gods, India, which is ourselves, shall enter upon these lines in the persons of us, her living sons. We shall take these little boys who are the citizens of the future India, and educate them upon ancient models, so that they shall be trained as India's boys should be. We shall bring them under the influence of the old inspiration, so that when they become heads of households, they shall be examples of what Indian husbands and fathers should be. We will hold up before them the ideal of honoured old age, respected, loved, reverenced by all. In the plastic years of youth, we shall hold up this ideal before them; nay, we shall ourselves live the ideal before them, imperfectly though it may be. They will work it out better; with better opportunities, they will produce nobler models; and the next generation will be higher still, and the generation succeeding it will be loftier still, and thus a new India will be built up generation after generation. But the foundation shall be laid now without delay, without putting it off to the future; we will lay the foundation, we, the living people of modern India, without shrinking from what it costs us; we will lay the foundation, and on that our boys shall build, and on their work our grand-children shall build, and on that again our great-grand-children, and thus shall be made a noble, purer, and more spiritual India."

Such an India will be fit to be the spiritual teacher of all nations. Such an India will be the Brâhmaṇa of humanity, her voice the voice of the Gods. That is the glorious ideal of which I call you to lay the foundation. Set you firm the stones on which the edifice shall rest, and they who come after us shall build the temple above them.

Lecture II.

TEMPLES, PRIESTS, AND WORSHIP.

Brothers :—

If you look back to India twenty-five years ago, you will be struck with the fact that the growing youths of India at that time were very largely materialised through the influence of purely secular and Western training; that the tendency of the intelligent men of the time was to turn more and more away from their ancestral faith, and to take as their prophets Huxley, Spencer, Mill, and Hegel, rather than the great Ṛishis of the past. That tendency, fatal to all spiritual life, and therefore to the very life of India herself, has now most happily been checked; and we find, as we look round the young men of the day, that there is more and more inclination among them to learn about their religion, to respect the great Scriptures, to regard the past with the reverence that is its due, and to nurse some dawning hopes of the revival of past spirituality and past glory. That change is so clear, so marked, so indisputable, that it is recognised on all hands alike; some speak of it with rejoicing, others with disapproval. But whether it be looked at by friend or by foe, by those who praise or by those who blame it, there is equally the recognition of the fact. On that point no challenge, no dispute arises.

Side by side with this great revival of Hinduism, there has, of course, been a revival also of some things that are regrettable; for evil follows good as the shadow follows the body, and we know from the highest authority, that all actions are enveloped in evil, as fire is surrounded by smoke. It is one of the conditions of action in an imperfect world that evil shall ever tread on the heels of good, and all that we can hope to do is to get the preponderance of good. If we expect undiluted good, then we are doomed to disappointment. We must be content to win the most good with the least possible evil, and if we succeed in that, we shall have served our generation well.

It is equally clear, I think, that all who take part in that great revival of religion, in however humble a way, must also do their utmost to minimise any evils which may follow on its progressive path. Those who have a share in the work of recalling the

Indian people to their great ideals, and of striving to fan into flame the smouldering spark of spiritual life, have certainly the duty of giving warning of the dangers that attend on the revival, of trying to check abuses, at the same time that they stimulate religious fervour and true spirituality.

Religion has two great enemies, that have ever accompanied it along its path throughout the history of humanity—materialism on the one side, superstition on the other. Both are dangerous to true religion; both hold weapons whereby to destroy the work of religion, to render her useless to mankind. Materialism stands out a pronounced and open enemy, with sword uplifted, trying to strike her down. Superstition more insidiously creeps up behind her, and veiling her own face in the mask of piety, offers the poisoned cup to her lips, striving to weaken, if not wholly to destroy. Those who are servants of religion must seek to guard her alike against the sword of the open foe and the poisoned cup of the secret enemy; for life may be destroyed whether by sword-thrust or by poison, and the faithful servant must guard the life of his mistress against both enemies, and warn the world of the double peril that assails her.

But in dealing with such a subject as that to which we turn our thoughts this evening, we are faced with the greatest and subtlest of difficulties. I know of no subject which is harder to deal with rightly, than the one to which we are now to devote our attention. Bound up as it is with all the feelings of reverence and devotion that ennoble and elevate humanity, sacred beyond all sacredness to those who know something of what lies beyond the visible, with the power of words too feeble to describe all that it includes, all that it indicates, how can one deal with those errors that injure it without seeming to touch the sacred ark in which the life of the nation is enclosed? There is a story in an ancient Hebrew Scripture that once the ark of the Lord was being taken along the road to its resting-place, and as the oxen drew the ark, some roughness in the road made it shake backward and forward, so that it seemed in peril of falling. A man, moved by hasty impulse, put forward rough and careless hand to touch the ark of the Lord. The motive was good, but the action mistaken; and as he touched the ark, the power of the life that was within it smote him, and he fell to the ground, senseless and slain, having touched unprepared the holy ark of Israel.* So great is the

* Objects which have been consecrated effectively are like very powerful batteries, and their contact is fatal to lives that cannot vibrate sympathetically. Hence the warnings to "the profane," meant only to protect them from danger.

danger of touching these arks of spiritual life, unless the hand be purified, unless the heart be devoted. May the great Gods protect me who speak and you who listen, lest, in our very desire of serving the great faith of our forefathers, any irreverence should enter our hearts and wrong that which we earnestly desire to serve.

If there were a great one whose limbs were loaded with fetters, who was chained so that he could not move to do his beneficent work, he would do a useful service who strove to file away the fetters that loaded his limbs and prevented them from moving. And so it may be that as in the course of thousands of years the great truths of Hinduism have become surrounded on some points by errors, by superstitions, and by evil practices, we may be able, with all reverence for truth, to file away the fetters that clog the limbs of this greatest of religions, and so set her free in modern days, as she was in the ancient, to bless all India with her power, and to draw the hearts of all men to herself. Just because the religion is so high, there is danger lest the errors encumbering her should injure more than if the religion were less lofty. A man who is standing on the ground cannot be much injured by a fall; but a man who has climbed up high may shatter his limbs in the falling. So it has ever been the case, that where the holiest is degraded, the most harm is done. the loftier and the greater the ideal, the more fatal is the degradation of that ideal in its injurious power over the hearts and lives of men.

What was the Temple in the ancient days? What the Image of the God? What the sacred shrine wherein It dwelt? What the holy places of pilgrimage, the Tîrthas whither men went to cleanse alike the body and the mind? What were all these in the wonderful past, when every priest was a true knower of the Supreme, and when the sacred Science of the Self shone in all its glory over the sacred land of India?

What the temple was in those ancient days those perhaps best can tell, who know what the Temples are to-day in the higher regions of the universe, the faint reflection of whose glory was once seen in the Temples of Hinduism, in the sounding of the mantras uttered by lips worthy to recite them.

What, then, was the Temple in those days? The Temple was the centre of Divine influence, the place where the presence of the Gods was known and felt, where the glory of the Gods would now and again shine forth in the eyes of the worshippers, and where the love of the Bhakta would draw down a visible manifestation of the compassion of Deity. Every one coming with love and devotion to such a Temple, found descending upon him a celestial influence, that calmed the mind, that elevated the spirit, that changed all thoughts of the world into thoughts of heaven, and that made prayer arise unchecked by any obstacle, so that the man felt for the time being as if he had entered within the very gates of Svarga. So mighty a power was there that even the most careless man who came there was for the moment changed and spiritualised, by the wondrous force which dwelt in the Temple, by the power radiated from the Image of the God within it.

Such was the consecration in the ancient days, when wisdom and purity were always present in the leaders, in the days when knowledge spoke the mantra, when none might come near the Temple as priest whose heart and lips were not purified with the Divine fire, when the priest who took the offerings of the faithful stood with outstretched hands that were pure, when every offering was sanctified by the love of the giver, and sanctified still further by the priest's hands as he took them to pass them on as offering to the Gods. So all alike were blest, and the holy influence radiated all around the Temple. Naturally men dreamed that in the Temple—and it was not all a dream—with the chanting of the mantras, the music of the Devas mingled its heavenly strain, and that worshippers unseen, but not unfelt, joined in the worship of men.

Such was the ancient Temple—a centre of spiritual life. And the Images that in those Temples stood to remind the worshippers of those mighty Ones—some of whose attributes were shown forth by symbols, by signs, by gestures—those great Images were full of that power, which, in its lowest form, we speak of as magnetic, but which, in its highest form, is a mighty spiritual force. For just as on the physical plane a man may take an object, may magnetise it and give it power to heal diseases by mere contact; so can great Ṛishis, servants of the high Gods, use the spiritual forces of which the physical magnetism is the faintest reflection, can pour that on the sacred Image, can vivify it, can give it mighty power, so that the vibrations coming from it harmonise everything that approaches it: the bodies of the worshippers—the subtle body as well as the physical—are thus made to vibrate rhythmically with those higher vibrations, and thus cease to be obstacles to the spiritual life, and serve instead as vehicles whereby the spirit may reach them. So great is the force of such an Image, so mighty the power that it can exercise over worshippers who come with faith and devotion, such the idea of what the Image of a God should be. Such in truth it was in the old days, and such it might be to-day.

Then there were the sacred Tîrthas to which men and women made pilgrimage, where they found some great Ṛishi, who, going down into the water, consecrated that water by his own spiritual influence and force, and gave it power which the bare water could by itself never have; who, by the pouring out of the spiritual life within him, imparted to the fluid the sacred power which affected the body, the mind, and the very spirit of those who went into it. In the ancient days, when the Ṛishi had done his consecrating work, his disciples went into the water after him, and then the crowd of pilgrims, treading with reverence, with solemnity, with dignity, entered into the flood thus rendered magnetic by the spiritual force poured out into it. Image to yourself those ceremonies of the past; see how they were pure, see how they were holy, see how no hard words were ever heard, how there was no roughness, no jostling—nothing that could disturb the sacred peace, the perfect harmony, of the place; and then you may dimly feel what pilgrimage meant in those days. Then you may dimly feel what power of holiness came down on men in such a place to raise them above the world in which they were living. You can catch some faint idea, and it can only be the faintest, of what the Gods can do for man, if man will only make the conditions that render it possible for Them to act: if they will but prepare the physical world, so that the celestial life may flow down into clean vessels, that will not pollute the holy flood that pours into them.

If in those days of the past, you could have attended one of the ancient sacrifices, if you could have been present at one of the ceremonies in those days when the priests who served at the altar were every one of them learned in the Vedas, every one of them pure in heart and in life—at such a ceremony what would you have seen? You would have seen earthly priests serving at the earthly altar; and then, if your eyes were open, you would have seen the high Gods who had come down in order to be partakers of the offerings that were laid on the altar. The great Ṛishis, the Sages, the mighty Ones of the older days came to bless those who were truly worshipping, to give the celestial benediction to the sacrifice that was pure, and to the worshippers who were worthy to receive it. Vast hosts of heavenly visitors and heavenly choristers, singing in harmony with the mantras sung below, and rain of flowers—celestial flowers—as the sign that the sacrifice was accepted, that the Gods were well pleased. So great was this religion in its older days, a copy of that which is mightiest in the unseen world: its Temples models of celestial Temples, its ceremonies a reflection of the ceremonies by which the spiritual evolution of the world is carried on, its priests representatives of that high priesthood who in the very presence of the Gods perform the Yajña and the Yoga by which alone the races of men are led along the path of the higher life, and are guided from the state of the brutes to the state of the Gods themselves. This religion of Hinduism is the nearest copy of that divine ritual that exists on earth, given to man more perfectly modelled by the Gods themselves than is the case with any other faith that has been given to human race, and therefore is Hinduism dear to the heart of the occultist. Divine in its ideas, sacred and spiritual in its ceremonies, with all the mighty powers of the Gods within it, that is the religion which your fathers have bequeathed to you. What have you done with that inheritance, Oh! you who boast yourselves their children?

Nor was that great and magnificent ritual and public religious life the only thing that they gave to their beloved sons and daughters of the Indian land. They came into the family, as they came into the Temples. They gave them Gurus to teach them, to guard from dawn to sunset the life of men and women, to guide from conception to cremation. They gave to the family, Gurus who should lead them step by step along the sacred path of life. There was no incident in the life that was not consecrated by the touch of the Guru's hand. He gave the second birth, while the father and mother gave the physical birth only, and so was this the highest and most sacred of all earthly ties—the tie between the Guru and the Shishya. It was the holiest of all charges, the charge placed in the Guru's hand to train the soul, to guide the feet along the ancient narrow path, sharp as the edge of the razor.

Such was the Guru in the olden days. Such his place in the family. Such his help to those to whom he was sent. Nor may the Purohita be ignored, who performed the household ceremonies of religion, as the Guru gave the training to the soul. He also was wise and pure, he also learned and noble. If I name the name of Vasiṣhṭha, I name one of those who was household priest in the elder days.

Such, then, was this mighty religion, nay, a million times more than this, if only I had words whereby to tell it. No thought of yours can paint a picture more divine than was once seen in ancient India. All words fail in telling of its beauty, all language is cold to describe the glory of its power.

What are the Temples now, and what their servants? What the Images and the Tîrthas? What the family Guru, and the family Purohita? Let us, remembering that great ideal, touch with careful hands all that represents it, but none the less let us see whether there do not exist to-day evils of the gravest character which are preventing the work of this great religion, which are alienating the minds of some of the brightest children of India from their ancestral faith, which are weapons whereby those who believe not in this faith try to turn men's heart against it.

I know, and you know it also too well, that when those who are not Hindus in belief speak of Hinduism, they do not speak of the glory of its Scriptures, or of the greatness of its philosophy, or of the wonders of its spiritual devotion; they do not dwell on all these great things which cannot be separated from any true view of Hinduism. They take up certain abuses, they point to scandals that dishonour ancient fanes and pollute holy places; and bringing those out into the light of day, they make them stand as the marks of this holy religion. We cannot answer them, alas! we cannot answer them, because their reproaches are based on facts that we know to be true.

Temples throughout modern India: how far does the old consecrating influence still live in them to-day? In some it is still found. In going into some of the Indian Temples, one feels coming down into them—even in the outer courts, where stand those who are not Hindus by birth, and who are therefore not permitted to enter the sanctuary —one feels even there the holy influence which once was so potent; but it is faint and feeble, as though preparing to depart and to be felt no more. I have been into some of the Temples here, where there is still some touch of the ancient power, still some vibrations of the ancient spiritual magnetism, still some influence that calms the mind and fills the heart with emotions of Bhakti, with love to God and man. But those Temples are few and far between, are in a small minority, instead of being everywhere as they were in the older days. In a vast number, there is no influence at all, no more than is in the world around them. In some, at least, the influence is of positive evil, and not of good, magnetism, where want of learning and want of purity have polluted the ancient magnetism that once dwelt therein.

Why? Because when this great blessing of spiritual force is given to any material object or place, it is not given as a force that remains there unchanged, no matter what the surroundings. It tends—as do all energies—gradually to dissipate; unless it is reinforced, unless it is renewed, it lessens in its potency. That there is still left some of it in these Temples is chiefly due to the crowds of pious worshippers who go thither to make their offerings to the Gods. Their love and their devotion reinforce the spiritual power that still remains in some holy places, and the possibility is thus shown of what might return, if duty were done on every hand.

What is true of the Temples is true of too many of the sacred Images. They, too, have lost their ancient power and no longer radiate much of the celestial energy; but still, when a man with a heart of love goes to bow down before such an Image, the God will send him blessing even though He dwells not there habitually. For love in the human heart attracts the love of the great Ones, and They answer, however unworthy the surroundings, where any soul of man is seeking after God.

And the Temple Brâhmaṇas? You know as I know, that both in the south and in the north, it is no word of reverence that springs to the lips when people speak about the Temple Brâhmaṇas. Have I not been told in southern India, by man after man, religious, devoted, at heart thoroughly Hindu, worshippers in the Temples, worshippers of the Gods, that their great difficulty is that their Temple priests are unlearned, that they are profligate in life, as well as unversed in the knowledge that should be theirs? Have they not complained, in bitter grief, that this is the great hindrance to religion, that shame is continually being brought upon them? Have they not prayed that some help may be given them to educate the priesthood, and to render those pure who serve the Gods? For if a man of evil life and foul thought stand beside the Image of a God, receiving the offerings that are made, the foulness of his magnetism pours out upon the sacred Image, and blasphemes it with a blasphemy worse a thousandfold than any attacks of missionaries can be; for no words of theirs can injure it much, but the ignorance and the impurity of the priests drive away the celestial energy.

Do we not know that the very names of Mahants and Pandâs carry to the ears of many who hear them associations of degradation and not of spiritual power, of shame and not of pride? Do we not know that if we stand at a sacred Tîrtha, we see there scenes that make us turn away in bitter shame, shocked at the rapacity of those who gather round the pilgrims, and who, in the very water that should be sacred to the blessed Gods, absolutely strive with each other physically to drag the pilgrims into their own hands, for the sake of money.

Can the Gods come down to such places? Why, there are Temples, where learned and devout Hindus will not allow the women of their families even to go. Can the Gods come down to places where women are not safe? Can the holy Ones descend, where shame is wrought in the name of piety and religion? My brothers, these are the scandals that are hindering the growth of Hinduism. They are known, they are whispered from one to another; they are the cankers of this great religion, and they are eating away its heart and turning against it its own children, who ought to be its most faithful lovers and most ardent admirers.

Do we not know that too often the family Guru is not even looked on with love and honour, not always because of Western education and falling away from religion, but because it is hard to give respect where there is nothing that is respectable. And that most sacred of all names, the name of Guru, has come to be a name that some men shrink from using to any teacher they revere, because of the shame that has been brought upon it by those who bear it unworthily.

If a man has in him a heart that is strong enough, a faith that is heroic enough, to look through the unworthy Guru to the great Guru, whose power may come down even through that unworthy channel; if a man has courage, devotion, and insight enough to disregard the unworthy form, and see in it merely a channel for the power that is divine; then the mantra given by even such a Guru will purify and spiritualise the man who takes it, and he will not suffer because the one who gave it was not worthy to be the giver. Do not, then, break the tie of love, the tie of duty, even when the representative is unworthy. Be patient for a little time. Bear with these unworthy ones for the sake of the ideal they represent, for the sake of the glory of the past, and for the holiness of the name that is cast as a veil over the unworthiness of the present. Remember that blessing will come to you even through these if you are worthy to receive it. But for those who thus prostitute the holiest of names, who by ignorance and profligacy blaspheme the most sacred of relations, for them there lies in the future the lowest of Narakas, the doom of those who have blasphemed the Divine in man, and have outraged that which is the holiest and the most pregnant with the salvation of mankind.

Do you dream, because you live in modern days, that these great things are but shadows of their former selves? Do you dream that they have lost their real force, that the great truths have lost their vital energy, that the holy mantras have now no power, that the sacred Scriptures have now no magic and no strength? The change is not in them, but in those who use them, in whose hands they are as forms empty of all life, these things which once brought down the very powers of God before the senses of men. I who speak to you, I bear you witness that these Scriptures, which are yours, but whose powers you know not, are still as mighty as ever they were in ancient days; that these mantras have still as much of the ancient power as ever, if only they are rightly uttered. For I know, that where sacred shlokas have been chanted by lips that were wise and pure, all that is said of the old days is true to-day, as really as ever it was in the past; even now to hear such chanting, the Devas throng from every quarter, making the air vibrant with the rustle of their celestial garments, filling the whole air with perfume, while the silver tinklings of the bells of the heavenly choristers chime in harmoniously with the sonorous chanting of the Samskrit shlokas by the priest. That still is true. It is not the form that is wanting; it is the life that should animate the form. There is the difficulty. It is that which we have to seek.

My brothers! is it possible for us to find out a remedy, without breaking the old ideals, and while keeping them still sacred? Is it possible to get rid of the abuses which are strangling them to death, and to give back to India what she once possessed?

I know well that it would be easy enough to sweep away all these abuses, for it would not take much to stir the Indian heart to anger, so that it should sweep them all away. But it would at the same time sweep away all the forms that need to be revivified, all the ideals, and not only the abuses. There is the difficulty that faces us. Better be patient, and bear much, working slowly for change, than break all the vessels which contain the possibilities of Indian spirituality for the future. It is easy enough by Acts and Laws to change the outer things, to stop the outer scandals. Easy enough by Acts, that might be passed by a Christian Government, to say that a man once convicted of crime should not be again placed on the gaddi. But are you sure that in that quick and hasty method of reform, you would not destroy the very thing that we must preserve, if India's spirituality is to survive? It is not always the outwardly quickest way that is the best way to take, especially in matters spiritual, which count time but little, which regard the ideal as vital. Therefore it is that in the lines that I suggest, I put on one side the rough and ready methods, whereby politicians correct political abuses, in matters where the conditions may be changed by enacting laws. The evil here lies deeper than any law can touch. The harm is rooted in regions in which no act can run. Slow must be the methods by which the deep change can be brought about. Can we not be patient in our workings, if we see the goal at which we aim?

Two things are chiefly wanted in order that the abuses I have spoken of may be cleared away. One is the slow method of education; the other a rise in the spirituality of the people, of the Hindus themselves. I know full well that these methods will not recommend themselves to those who are so angry with the evils that they see, that they would strike quickly, in order to get rid of them at once. I do not plead for the abuse, when I ask you to be patient in bearing it. The words of a wise Teacher of the ancient times should be remembered, when He told His disciples not to pull up too hastily the weeds that had grown along with the wheat, lest they should also pull up the young corn; but rather wait until the corn was strong enough to bear the movement around its roots, so that the weeds might be gathered and thrown into the fire, which was their proper place, without injuring the corn.

Education is the first thing wanted. When I speak of the ignorance of the priesthood, I refer to the priestly class spoken of above, and not, of course to those learned Pandits, profound in their scholarship, whose learning is a glory to their land, and who have kept alive Indian philosophy. I am not speaking of these great lights of modern India, but I speak of the Temple priests; that is where education must begin in order to strike at the very root of mischief. You must remember that significant declaration of Manu, when he said that "As an elephant made of wood, as an antelope made of leather, so is an ignorant Brâhmaṇa; these three have only the names." I have met many a Brâhmaṇa in southern India who was ignorant even of Saṁskrit, and who knew not the very meaning of the mantras that he repeated, even in the mere outward meaning of their words, far less the spiritual meaning that underlies them. I have seen Brâhmaṇas officiate at sacred ceremonies, who could not even pronounce aright their Saṁskrit words, and who used wrong words in the midst of the mantras, so taking away the little efficacy that they might have had, had they been rightly pronounced. Other words of Manu come to my mind, certainly not lacking in strength: "As a eunuch is unproductive with women, and a cow with a cow is unprolific, even so useless is the Brâhmaṇa who is not instructed in the Vedas." No words of mine are these, but words of that mighty Teacher who stands at the head of Hinduism, nay at the head of the present race. Shall we not then try to win the priests to submit to education? shall we not try to make it easy, so that education shall be open to them on every side? It is not for us to reform the priesthood; not from below may the purifying fire ascend. It is for the priesthood to reform itself, and this it will do if educated. The fire must come from the heart of the priestly community to purify it, otherwise the work will be ill-done and the results will be transitory and poor.

But there is already a movement in southern India among the religious Hindu community, and they have appealed to us here to lend them a helping hand in gaining a learned priesthood. Some of the Trustees of Temples have come and asked us whether it was not possible, in connection with this Central Hindu College, to open a Theological Department, where sons of priests might be trained and educated, and then go back to the Temples and take up their fathers' work, worthy to be servants of the high Gods. The working out of that plan is already in contemplation. There will be here made arrangements by which the sons of priests will be taken, supported by those who send them, in order that they may be trained in the elements of general morality and religion, and also in Western knowledge—for it is necessary that the priest should not be divided from the people, by knowing nothing of that which they know. And therefore it is proposed, with the approval of those who have spoken to us, that the boys should be first trained in the ordinary curriculum, and should then pass into the Theological Department, and there be trained further in Samskrit learning, as well as in the ceremonial knowledge pertaining to the duties of the priesthood. If that scheme be carried out, if the College here co-operate with our brothers in the south in this respect, surely that will be the beginning of brighter days. If we can send forth a learned priesthood, such a priesthood will be purer in life than if it is utterly ignorant, for with ignorance goes degradation. If that task can be accomplished here, then a great work will be done for India's future, when the priests thus trained will go back to the Temples that they serve, and there lead lives respected by the community, honourable, upright, pious, examples to those who throng to the Temples.

So, in other parts of India, similar movements might be begun. There is possibility of reform here. Let us then plead with the priests to educate themselves, let us make it easy for them to do it. There are plenty of funds contributed by pious people; why should not these be used for the benefit of the priesthood, so that the Temples may be served by learned and pious Brâhmaṇas? This is dealing with the very root of the evil. Is it not a thousand times better to do this, than to appeal to Government to pass Acts which simply cut off the heads of abuses while the roots remain untouched? Let us work patiently then, and within thirty years the priests will be changed without giving religious feeling a shock, without outraging its sensibilities,

That is not all. Every nation has as its teachers, the teachers that it deserves. If there are serving in the Temples many who have no right to be there, it is because of the low level of spirituality in the masses of the people. Karma gives to every nation that which that nation has earned. The priesthood given to India is fitted to the degraded spiritual life among her people. It is the way of the West to see the outer evils only and to try to destroy them. It is the way of the East to study the law of Karma, and to sow seeds that shall bring forth fair harvest. The interests of our lives are not centred in one life, as the West thinks; but we are taught that we are not bounded by these bodies, we are living life after life, and so we can afford to work for the future, as men work who know that their life goes on growing and evolving. Let us then turn our hearts and lives towards ancient ideals, let us begin by spiritualising ourselves, let us worship faithfully and with devotion, let us meditate daily, steadily, and perseveringly for spiritual fervour, let us purify our lives and learn charity, tenderness, love of all that is around us. Let us improve ourselves, and Karma will and must send us priests who will be worthy to serve at the altar and in the family. Let us trust the good Law, and the Gods behind every phenomenon; Their power is real, the power that guides all nations. Let us offer pure lives of devotion, and They will give us back as reward a pure priesthood, and teachers who are learned and spiritual men. Those two methods of change I venture to recommend to you—the education of the priesthood, and the raising of the standard of spirituality in the nation.

Let each man take this to himself, and not put it off on his neighbour. Let us not say, "India has sunk low;" but rather let us say, "I have sunk low, and I must rise." If every man says that, then India will rise. If each man will cultivate the vineyard of his own life, the whole area will be cultivated, and the blessings of the Gods will be once more upon the people.

So with regard to the family Guru and the family priests. Rather work hard and wait, than hastily break up and destroy. But there is one outer thing that you might fairly do. In every ceremony where choice is yours, when there are ceremonies to which you invite Brâhmaṇas, and you choose them from among the great mass around you, then without transcending your own proper duty, you could always choose only the learned and the pure. You should on such occasions leave on one side the illiterate and the profligate. Where choice is yours, why should you not choose the useful, instead of those that are branded as useless? Thus you will bring about some changes that will come more rapidly, without touching the holy ideals, that we all feel the necessity of preserving.

Still further, it seems to me, it may be possible to go. But here I speak with something of doubt, because of the exceeding difficulty of finding any person who has a right to move in the matter, of finding any recognised authority. Is it quite impossible that we might win the more thoughtful, the more learned of the priesthood, to join with us and give us their helping hand in stopping some of the worst scandals that go on around us day by day? Might it not be possible that a body of good Mahants and Pandâs should as a first step exclude from his office a Mahant or Pandâ who has been condemned by law for some shameful crime? I do not see any lack of readiness on their part to go to the Courts where their own interests are concerned, so that they already have recourse to the ruling power with regard to temporalities. We all know how the money offered to the Gods is squandered in courts, in litigating cases; and how the offerings of the faithful are spent on the law and the lawyers. We all know also, that priests themselves sometimes mortgage away their rights to receive such offerings, and that the offerings of Hindus, intended to support their religion, go to persons outside Hinduism, to those who are not even of the Hindu faith. It does not seem impossible, therefore, that the same power might be invoked by the more worthy of the priests to redress flagrant scandals, to interfere with and prevent unworthy priests from continuing to receive emoluments belonging to their office. It does not seem impossible that the honourable men might make a tribunal whose voice should be recognised as authoritative by the civil government, so that when it pronounced a man unworthy, its decision should be recognised as barring him from bringing a suit to claim any place in a Temple, or any maintenance, or proprietary rights. It seems to me not impossible that such a thing might be done. Applied first to a man condemned by the law for a crime, it might be applied gradually, as the standard rises, to less flagrant cases. But this plan can only be worked out by those who are learned alike in religion and in law. I can only in this give hints and suggestions. It is for wise and learned Hindus to see if anything can be done practically in this direction, without injuring the ideal of a true priesthood, and without destroying anything that is worthy of preservation.

If some such immediate changes can be brought about, and if the growing spirituality of the people and improved education raise the status of the priesthood, if these purifying forces go on, step by step, then it would seem that brighter days will dawn again for Hindu faith and Hindu practice.

[Apart from the ignorance and the immorality of the priesthood, there are other things that need to be changed in connection with some few of the Temples, though happily only found in comparatively few—animal sacrifice and nautch-girls.

I know well—perhaps better than many of those who defend it—the hidden truth out of which animal sacrifice has arisen. But the slaying of animals as now performed is utterly indefensible, and the shedding of their blood pollutes and defiles the Temples where it takes place. Asuric are these animal sacrifices of the Kali Yuga, "tormenting the aggregated elements forming the body, and Me also, seated in the inner body," and they should be entirely discontinued.

So with the nautch-girls. Originally there existed in connection with the Temples a band of pure maidens, vestal virgins, through whose unsullied lips, from time to time, a God or a great Ṛishi would speak, warning or teaching the worshippers. Only a pure virgin could serve as such a vehicle, for the temporary embodiment of a great One whose physical body was far away. These virgins were guarded with the greatest care, and were looked on with the greatest reverence. Theirs it was to serve the priests ministering at the shrine and to weave the mystic dance with sacred garlands, moving to the measure of the music that they chanted, amid the fragrant smoke of incense, as the stately procession moved from fane to fane.

As the priests degenerated they dragged down the Temple maidens with them, until now their name carries with it only suggestions of shameful vice. Little wonder that all good influences have fled where womanhood is thus degraded, and the highest spiritual uses have been changed into lowest sin.]

Is it all a dream, impossible of realisation, that Indian Temples shall again be what once they were; that Indian sacred Images again shall have their divine power; that Indian priests shall again be what they ought to be—models for those for whom they minister; that Gurus shall be wise, pious, and learned, worthy to train their Shishyas along the path of wisdom, virtue, and piety? Is this only a Utopian dream?

My brothers, I cannot think it. For in this land there still remains what no other land in the world possesses. There is still a spiritual life hidden within the hearts of men. There are still places where it makes itself felt. There are still spots which are holy, and which are kept holy for the sake of the future, that yet shall be born. There is still in the hearts of the Indian people a spiritual fibre that elsewhere is not found. There is still response from them to a spiritual appeal, that no other nation in the world is as yet able to give. Is all that to be wasted? all these to be lost, at the very moment when Indian thought is penetrating the world? Is India herself to be excluded from that great life, that through her is pouring out to the nations of the West? That need not be; that shall not be.

If only India's children will do what they should do, by virtue of the past behind them, by virtue of the Gods above them, by virtue of the great Ṛishis who still live, and who love their ancient fatherland, who even in their high estate turn eyes of tenderest love on India's children, and welcome them with a greater joy than they welcome the children of other lands—then shall India rise. I cannot believe that India has no future, that this greatest of all faiths has no revival possible, which shall place her on the pinnacle where all the world shall worship her, as a mighty power for spirituality.

Surely she shall, despite all, be the mother of spiritual races yet unborn.

I dream of a time when Temples again shall be centres of spiritual life, when the sacred mantras shall ring out again in all their purifying, harmonising force, when the language of the Devas shall regain its ancient power, when the hearts of men shall bow in worship before the great Gods who rule over mankind, and before the Divine Teachers who are their nearest Priests. Of that I dream, my Brothers.

And I know that even if this dream be but a dream—which may the Gods forbid—even then it is good to work for spiritual regeneration. Whether this dream be true or not, no force can be wasted, no change that is for good can be lost. Spirituality growing here shall cause spirituality to grow all the world over. Even if the crown of spirituality may not be India's, nay, may go elsewhere, those who work for her to-day will be content that somewhere there will rise a spiritual Teacher before whom all the world shall bow in homage. That spiritual Teacher may wear an Indian body, may be in the likeness of the Ṛishis of old; for that I pray the Gods, for that I work, for that I give the life that now I hold. And I pray you that you also will give your lives, you who have the privilege of

Hindu birth, which in this life I have not, you who can go into the Temples where I may not go, who may worship where I may not worship. I am pleading for that which should be dearer to you than it is to me. Will you be deaf to the pleadings of love, and let India perish, as she must perish, if her religion dies?

LECTURE III.

THE CASTE SYSTEM.

MY BROTHERS:—

We are to study to-night that characteristic system of caste, which we find in India from the very earliest days of the Áryan civilisation, which has persisted in its form down to the present time, and which is probably the chief reason for the stability of Indian Society. In studying this system we shall proceed along the same lines that we have hitherto followed. First we shall look at it in its state of perfection; then we shall see it as it has degenerated until it reached its present position; then we shall consider whether any changes are practicable which should restore it to its former usefulness and glory, and deprive it of the many disadvantages and mischiefs at present connected with it.

Any subject that deals with the social life of a people needs very careful consideration, and suggestions of the introduction of any changes must be made with the greatest caution, with the greatest deliberation. Therefore, in dealing with the latter part of this subject, I shall put before you tentatively certain propositions, which may serve, at least as the basis for discussion, even if not accepted in the form in which they are originally presented.

It seems to me necessary, in dealing with a point of this kind, and with all questions like this, that we should distinguish very clearly between that which is essential and that which is non-essential. That is, we must divide our subject into those parts which are vital, those parts which are permanent, and the parts which are non-essential, which are temporary, which do not spring out of the original principles, but have to do with the more modern conditions—accretions that have grown up around the system, and which by no means are essential to its vitality, but rather detrimental to its life.

Now, as regards the original idea of the caste system, it is laid down exceedingly carefully and clearly among many other passages in the *Bhagavad-Gîtâ*, Fourth Discourse; here Shrî Krishna Himself says: "The four castes were emanated from Me by the different distribution of energies and actions; know Me to be the author of them."

That is a distinct declaration from the lips of Shrî Kṛiṣhṇa Himself, as to the origin of the system. He puts Himself forward as the author, and He states that the division rests on certain fundamental principles in Nature, and follows a certain distribution of qualities, or energies, and actions. We find, if we take the terms there used, that it is the distribution of the Guṇas and the Karmas that determine castes; these are the essential fundamental qualities in Nature, and the actions arising from them which cause certain inevitable results. On these two things the four castes, He declares, are based. They are not, according to this, arbitrary distinctions; they are not, according to this, artificial creations of Society. They are fundamental *natural* divisions, based on differences of materials, based on resulting differences of actions. Such is declared, by the mouth of the Great Teacher, to be the foundation of the four castes.

In many other passages we find the same idea worked out. Some of the great Teachers give certain qualities, as characteristic of each of the four castes. Some go so far as to say, that if these qualities do not exist in a man, born in any particular caste, then he is not really a member of that caste. To take a case from the *Mahâbhârata*. After reciting the qualities belonging to a Brâhmaṇa, and the qualities belonging to a Shûdra, the teacher declared: "If these qualities are seen in a Shûdra and are not found in a Brâhmaṇa, then that Shûdra is not a Shûdra, nor is that Brâhmaṇa a Brâhmaṇa." So we see, that this view of the system is put forward: that there are certain fundamental differences in Nature, and the caste system being based on these, should show out the same characteristic differences.

If we study the system carefully, we shall find that these four castes present the path of Evolution, along which a human Soul develops. We shall find, in fact, that these fundamental divisions are by no means peculiar to Hinduism, are not only to be found in India, but that they are universal in their nature; they are recognisable over the whole of the countries of the world. The difference that we see between India and the other States of the West is simply this: that in the Hindu system these differences are recognised, and Society is definitely organised on their basis; while in the other countries these differences are not definitely recognised, and the social order is not connected with them.

Where you get a system in which these differences are recognised, and the social order is based upon them, it is spoken of as a system of castes.

Where you have a society without this recognition, but where the qualities assert themselves in spite of the ignoring of them, we speak of a system of classes. But the lines are easy to be seen, and may be definitely recognised. And you find in all past civilisations, as well as in the present civilisation, the same lines of cleavage, the same natural fundamental distinctions.

Now, in the definite recognition of these lines of cleavage, there is a distinct social value. It tends towards the stability of society, it tends to contentment, to the absence of continual competition and strife, and it makes society orderly and progressive at the same time. It is not without significance, that in one of the social Utopias, which have been sketched in the West, we find a system of society—outlined by the great French Philosopher Auguste Comte, whose philosophy is called the Positive Philosophy, and who founded on that philosophy the re-organisation of society—it is not without significance, that the caste system is there definitely revived, and the characteristic marks imprinted on it by Hindu Sages are found reappearing in this latest offspring of Western politico-social thought. We have there a well-organised priestly class, on the lines of the caste of Brâhmaṇas. I have not time to tell you the details of that system, of which one note is the mystical one of organising in sevens. But it is important that the man at the head of that class is to appoint one of his fellow priests as his successor, so that the authority is always from above and never from below. The whole control over commerce is to be in a class corresponding to that which we here call the Vaishya caste—great capitalists, who organise labour; and again, in a separate body, we have the proletariat, representing the Shûdra caste. The only caste that does not appear in this Utopia, is the Kshattriya, because the whole of this system is based on the supposition that society will be peaceful. There being an absence of war, there is no need for a military class. We have thus a definite caste system re-established on purely scientific lines, and the motto of the Positive Society is "Order with Progress." This is the same fundamental notion as we have in connection with the great Indian system of caste.

The next thing to remember is that this system, as regards the soul, is a great educative system. Re-incarnation is always implied in it. The soul passes from one caste to another, according to the qualities it has developed, according to the actions it has performed. It may rise upwards, or it may sink downwards, but always the effect of one birth shows itself in another birth, and the soul is led, stage by stage, along the pathway of evolution. And very plainly is this shown when you look upon the caste system in its pure form. The higher the caste, the greater the restrictions, the heavier the duties, the more burdensome the weight of responsibility placed on its shoulders. This system in its original form was not a system of rights claimed *by* a caste, but a system of duties imposed *on* a caste; the higher the caste, the heavier the duties..

As you study it, you find that the easiest life, the life with the least responsibility, with the least difficulty, with the least restriction, was the life of a member of the lowest caste, and not of the highest. As a man rose from one caste to another, as the soul grew older and stronger, he was made to resign more and more. Every restriction that was put upon a man was put on him in order to make him of greater service, and not to minister to his vanity or pride. If the Brâhmaṇa were surrounded with respect, it was on his shoulders that lay the burden of renunciation and sacrifice, of poverty and learning. All these restrictions were not made that he might be separated from the people, and pride himself on his separateness; but that he might be kept pure as a channel through which Divine life might flow to the people. And a man could only pass into that caste, when he had learned the lesson of sacrifice; when he had learned to serve as a Shûdra, when he had learned to give and be charitable as a Vaishya, when he had learned to sacrifice life itself as a Kshattriya; then, when he had become a lover of asceticism and learning, then was he permitted to pass into the order of Brâhmaṇas, to give himself to the people as their teacher, counsellor, and guide. That was the original idea of the system, that the kind of way in which the system worked.

It is well that you should be aware in connection with it that a certain definite type of subtle body belonged to each caste. According to the qualities, we read, the castes were emanated. But the qualities are expressed in the subtle invisible bodies, and the type of each caste is marked in the nature of the invisible bodies that belong to it. The Sûkshma Sharîra—the subtle body—was different in the four castes, was built up according to the qualities of each special caste, so that four types of Sûkshma Sharîras belonged to the four castes, and the qualities were expressed in appropriate organisms, and had each their appropriate vehicle, in which they could manifest.

What, then, was the part which heredity played in this system? Heredity was the obvious, necessary way of providing suitable physical bodies to suit each type of subtle bodies, in which the qualities were manifested. It was necessary to build up by physical heredity the kind of physical body which should answer to the type of the invisible body; and so heredity became a part, a necessary part, of this system, in order that the physical body might be suited to the subtle body, that the whole of the man might be consistent, and that there might not be incongruity between the subtle and the gross vehicles. How enormous was the difficulty of changing from one caste to another, you may estimate by the famous and well-known case of Vishvâmitra. If you realise this difference of bodies, then you will be able to understand why it was so difficult for a man to pass from one caste to another. Vishvâmitra having been born in the Kshattriya caste, with the Sûkshma Sharîra of the Kshattriya, and the physical body fitted by Kshattriya heredity to serve in correspondence with that subtle body, it was by no means an easy thing for him to change from the caste of Kshattriyas into the caste of Brâhmaṇas. It needed, you may remember, a process of Yoga, prolonged through an enormous number of years, in order to make the necessary changes in those bodies, which might render the transition possible. It was not a thing of a day or a month or a year; it was not that a man should merely show the qualities of the higher order; but it was only definite yogic practices prolonged through enormous periods of time, by which changes were made in the type, which rendered it possible for the Gods to greet him with the title of a Brahmârshi. Looking backwards, we cannot but recognise these fundamental types, these great lines of cleavage, and the place of heredity as an essential part of the system, in the well-organised arrangement of the whole. [A man who did not perform the dharma of his caste, and thus made a discord between the invisible and visible bodies, was, in the old days, outcasted, and thus the purity of caste was maintained. Thus suitable physical bodies were continually produced by heredity, and pure heredity was protected by outcasting.] Thus studying, we begin to see how and why this system was formed, how and why it has given to Indian Society such remarkable stability.

Further than this, we may notice that, from a true Hindu's standpoint, one particular life in a body was not regarded of such great importance, as it is now generally regarded in modern India.

A man who, by his past, was born in a body of a particular caste, did not look upon that as a matter of such vital import, as people are inclined to do in these degenerate days. The man took the karma of his body with perfect cheerfulness, knew it was only for a short time, was content to accept it for that time, and to build for himself a better body in the future, if he found that in the past he had built a body which was unsatisfactory to him. You find a man, in any order, willingly taking up the duties of that order and discharging them with contentment, and recognising his place in the Commonwealth. If I wanted to give an example, I might take the very speaker of *Bhagavad Gîtâ*, Shrî Kṛiṣhṇa Himself, who having chosen to be born in the caste of a Kshattriya because that was the best body for the work which was to be done, never dreamed of asserting His own inner superiority, His own divine nature, but willingly bowed down and washed the feet of Brâhmaṇas, showing an example which was due from the body which He had chosen to take, and which was appropriate to the situation which He held in life. I say that, in order that this old view may be before you, in its various aspects, and that you may realise how, in those days, when the spiritual laws were better understood, the castes worked without rebellion or discontent on the part of any member, however great or low his position, for it was recognised that all souls passed through all castes in turn; that if a man was born in a low caste to-day, he had only to evolve a higher nature, in order to be born in a higher caste hereafter. Men did not look on birth as a matter of chance, but as a matter of law, and they accepted the working of the Good Law, and conformed themselves to its provisions.

Gradually, however, a change arose. This system, originally founded and worked by great Ṛishis, the different castes inhabited by souls of strongly marked and different characteristics, worked well enough in those days. But as less and less developed souls were born into the system, their qualities no longer coincided with the special caste into which they were born. Less and less evolved souls came into Indian bodies, for training and instruction, and were no longer able to fulfil the dharma of the caste in which they were born. Then began the time of the multiplication of castes, and the subdivisions of the original four great orders. Men who could not show out the qualities, which in themselves would win the respect generally due to their caste, began inventing artificial barriers, by which they might separate themselves from others. Not showing out any difference in the soul, they laid more and more stress on social and personal advantages; they built up wall after wall, they built up distinction after distinction, to extort respect where their qualities did not naturally win it, and so introduced artificial distinctions, which were not present in nature, and had no basis in the facts of life.

Then there grew up these endless subdivisions, which are the great and very baneful characteristics of the caste system in the modern days—hundreds upon hundreds of sub-castes, effacing the original order, hundreds of sub-castes blurring all the natural lines, and resting on unreal, unnatural, purely artificial foundations, increased in their number by vanity and pride, continually multiplied by the spirit of exclusiveness, as mcn lost sight of the unity of the Self, and forgot that the Four Castes were the four ways of expressing His qualities. Thus, multiplied by this spirit of difference and separateness, the numbers of sub-castes and sub-divisions grew more and more. · Exclusiveness grew up in the heart. A man prided himself on the particular sub-division in which he was born, and put out his brothers, excluding them from his own sub-division, and ever striving to multiply distinctions, as separateness grew ever more plainly marked.

Hence we find to-day that the spirit of caste is essentially a spirit of exclusiveness, a spirit of pride and vanity, of indifference to the feelings of others, of harshness and contempt towards those who are excluded from special privileges. We find in it an indifference to the feelings of those who are shut out, and instead of a man thinking that he was born a Brâhmaṇa in order that he should serve those around him, he prides himself on being a Brâhmaṇa, in order to stand apart from them and above them, claiming for himself privileges and distinctions that they are not allowed to acquire. At the same time that this has been done the dharma of the caste has been utterly neglected. That a man should be poor and learned, that used to be the glory of a Brâhmaṇa. But in modern days, that he should be rich and ignorant is generally his pride. Instead of finding the Brâhmaṇa versed in the Vedas, you find him pleading in the Law Courts and versed in the western civilisation. Can you wonder that when the dharma of the caste is thrown aside, the respect which was once shown to the caste should also at the same time disappear? Can you wonder that when a Brâhmaṇa has abandoned his duty, others should refuse to him the privileges that he still claims? When you cannot distinguish him by his qualities from the Shûdra, why should he be treated with respect by the Shûdra? Can you wonder that the Shûdra should revolt against the superiority claimed, but not manifested, against the privilege extorted instead of being gladly given to well-acknowledged merit? Where a Brâhmaṇa is found who is as he ought to be—learned, frugal, wise, pure in heart, all men are still willing to show him reverence, to bow down to him and recognise him as a leader and teacher. Men are not, as a rule, unwilling to recognise excellence. Men are sometimes but too ready to be led, too glad to be guided. The human heart is always seeking for some one to lead it, some one to teach it, some one to guide it; and how exceedingly strong is this yearning in humanity may be seen in the pitiful spectacle of crowds bowing down to sorry heroes and heroines, not worthy of their respect, for lack of true heroes of the right kind. When we find in Indian Society to-day continual complaints against Brâhmaṇas, a feeling of anger, a feeling of jealousy, a feeling of envy, a desire to throw all castes aside, we should see in that the result of the fact that men are unreasonably demanding respect where others are unwilling to yield it; that men demand every privilege, forgetful of every duty, and that where privilege is grudgingly yielded, resentment grows up in the place of reverence and of love.

[From time to time it was as though the Gods themselves protested against the growing degeneracy and falsehood of the system, by sending some of the noblest souls to take birth in low-caste bodies, or even in those out of caste altogether. Thus several of the holiest and most revered saints in Southern India wore the bodies of pariahs.]

Let us also remember, in connection with this, the distinction between the essential and the non-essential, of which I spoke in the beginning. The essential is the great four-fold division, because this is founded in Nature. The non-essential is the innumerable artificial sub-divisions, chiefly founded on vanity and on the spirit of exclusiveness. Let us then separate, in our thought, the four-fold system of caste from the hundreds of sub-castes that we see around us on all sides; and let us lay down as one possible line of improving the present system, the recognition of the four-fold division only, and the gradual ignoring of those hundreds of sub-divisions that have arisen. Now, on this point, an authority worthy of all respect in the orthodox Hindu community has spoken clearly and distinctly. In Southern India there is at the head of one of the great Maths one who holds the honoured name of Shrî Shankarâchârya—a name which has come down as that of the head of that Math from the time of the great teacher of Advaita—who is recognised as the man who stands as the head of the whole religious community, and whose words are listened to with reverence by the whole body of the Southern Hindus. Only a few years ago, speaking with all the weight of that authority, he declared that the Hindus should drop this modern system of sub-castes, and that, within the limit of each caste, there should be inter-marriage and inter-dining. All Brâhmaṇas should be willing to inter-marry with all Brâhmaṇas and to inter-dine with all Brâhmaṇas. And so with the other three castes. In recommending this change I am therefore but repeating what has been suggested by one of the recognised orthodox authorities. This change is in no way detrimental to Hinduism, but is necessary to meet the conditions of modern days. It is not the four great divisions that raise so much antagonism, but these lines of artificial sub-division that separate man from man, and split the whole Indian community into small fragments and associations. These sub-divisions go against the possibility of national spirit, against the growing up of social unity; they make it almost impossible to weld the people into one; for where a community is divided into innumerable parts, all possibility of national and social unity disappears.

Supposing one of the possible reforms to be, that we put forward this idea of preserving the four-fold order, but gradually abolishing the numerous sub-divisions; might it not be possible to win the educated opinion of India to that idea, and so gradually to restore some vitality to this system? Might it not be possible that these innumerable sub-divisions should be gradually abolished, without shaking the foundation of the four-fold order which Shrî Kriṣhṇa declared to be established by Himself.

Then a question is continually raised—Can there not be transition from caste to caste? I cannot but ask you in answer: Where would the authority be found which would be capable of guiding such a transition, and would be recognised by all as truly authoritative? Frankly speaking, I do not believe that it is practicable, until a great authority, a true spiritual authority, is once more manifested and recognised through India, which will speak with the Divine Voice, and be able to give the recognition which is based on knowledge. You may remember that in the famous case of Vishvâmitra, before mentioned, it was not a recognition from those around him that he sought, but a recognition from the Gods Themselves, and from no lower authority. It was only when They proclaimed him a Brahmârshi, that the transition was recognised; and only true spiritual knowledge would be able to decide on such a point. Rather would I suggest the old and wise way of looking at this matter, that whatever be the body one is born with, one should, cheerfully accepting the karma of that body, work in that body with all its advantages and disadvantages, whatever they may be. If a bad body be what is obtained by one's karma, then one should cheerfully pay the kârmic debt and hope for a better body in the future. If the soul has taken a lower body than that to which his qualities entitle him, then it is proper to apply to such a case the theory that the soul has made the sacrifice for the sake of rendering some service to humanity; and having made the sacrifice, why should he grudge the payment of that sacrifice, and why should he not accept the karma of that body, and willingly take upon himself all the disadvantages it may entail? If we were more spiritual in our vision, and not so limited by the illusion of the body, we should not lay so much stress on these bodily distinctions, but should cheerfully accept the working of the Law and follow where the Law may lead.

Now we come to another fundamental point, one of the most practical we can consider. In the old days, there was a definite discipline in each caste. How was that discipline exercised? In the old days, outcasting was the instrument of discipline. What were the causes of which outcasting was the effect? This was necessary, as we have seen, in order to maintain the purity of the caste. Where the qualities of the caste were not shown, there the man was outcasted, and was not allowed to injure the family heredity by passing on the type of a body polluted by his evil qualities. There is still that old machinery, there is still that old name of outcasting, but the question arises to-day: By whom is that authority used? On whom is that authority exercised? Those who wield the authority of caste, are by no means, in the present day, for the most part, the true leaders of the caste, in learning, in wisdom, in purity, in the respect of their fellows. I speak what many of you know to be the fact, that over and over again, when decision is given in one of these caste sub-divisions, that decision is brought about by those who are by no means the worthiest members of that caste. It is largely a matter of intrigue and private interest, a matter of active exertion by some who have personal motives behind the work that they are doing; this is a well-known fact, and too often the decision of a caste is swayed by men who by outer formality of religion gain an outer respect, not warranted by purity of life, by learning, by wisdom and nobility of character. You know, further, as well as I do, that when you come to deal with outcasting, as now practised, it is not only that the people who practically control the decision are those who ought not to do it, but also that they exercise their authority over those over whom that authority should not be exercised. You know perfectly well that within the limits of caste a man may outrage every principle of morality, and yet no man will think of outcasting him. In life he may practically disregard all the caste principles, but if he keeps up an outward show, he is not outcasted. That man may go to a hotel, may eat beef, may get drunk; but provided he goes in by the back door and not by the front door, his caste-men will shut their eyes to his errors. Whereas if a man travels out of India, however well educated he may be, however pure the life he may lead, however useful he may be to his community, you will find that in some sub-divisions of a caste, he is outcasted for the mere fact of travelling. How can a system last where such injustice is done? If a young man leaves his country and goes abroad, when he returns, it is a mere question of chance whether he should be outcasted or not. Some men, when they have come back, have again been received by their caste-men, while others have not been. I do not wish to mention any names, but I could quote name after name of men who have travelled abroad, and are known to have so travelled, and who have been received by their own caste with welcome on their return. And I could also quote you a long number of names of those who have been treated in exactly the opposite way, who have been outcasted on their return, although no challenge has been made against their morality except that they have crossed "the black water." Sometimes a Vaishya goes abroad, comes back, and is welcomed in his caste; while in another case a Vaishya goes and is outcasted on his return. Only the other day in Calcutta, a Shrâddha was performed in which five hundred orthodox Brâhmaṇas were present. And yet it was the Shrâddha of the father of a man who had taken a degree in Europe, while there are many who, for the same reason, have been outcasted and shut away from all sacred rites. I know of two Brâhmaṇas of Southern India, one of whom was taken back into caste, and the other outcasted.

You must distinguish here between the question of travelling and the question of the result of European life on some of those who go, a result arising out of the evil conditions under which they live in Europe. That is quite a different matter, and should not be dealt with under this head; I will speak of that presently.

Let me speak to you for a moment on this question of travelling itself, which is moving young India more and more. You know that in the army, recruiting goes on largely among Brâhmaṇas; now every soldier has to take the oath to serve abroad, as well as here, but no one dreams of outcasting soldiers when they return from foreign service, though the same Brâhmaṇas would be out-casted if they had travelled abroad as civilians. There is no rational basis, no recognised standard, no real judgment, in such matters. Is it not true that, according to the ignorance of the sub-caste is the cruelty of its outcasting; the less the sub-caste is educated, the more bigoted is it with regard to this particular question.

In the old days, Indians were not tied down within the limits of India; Indians went freely out from India and travelled in the different countries of the world. You find stories of ship-wreck, curious incidents in foreign lands, showing that in those days Indians travelled freely in all directions, and no man dreamed of making the fact of travelling an accusation against his fellow Hindu. Not only was that the case in the past; it is the case to a considerable extent, even in the present, in some sub-castes. A large number of Vaishyas are travelling through Persia, following out their business, on matters of commerce. Large numbers of Southern Indians, of all castes, are travelling to and living in Burma at the present time, and are forming there a definite Hindu community, where all ordinary Hindu customs are observed and marriages are carried out. You find both in the past and in the present that Hindus travelled into foreign parts, and no man injured them because of it.

But this is not the only thing to consider. I ask you whether, in modern times, it is not clearly a part of the advancing march of the world that nations should mingle with nations, and learn to know each other better than they have done? Can you not see, on all sides, that nations are being drawn together, that walls of separation are being broken down, that they are learning to know each other, to understand each other, and so preparing to live together more peacefully than in the past? Over and over again, war breaks out through misunderstanding; where nations are separated from nations, they suspect each other, they mistrust each other, they hate each other, until such suspicion, mistrust, and hatred break out into international conflict. When nations know each other better, they learn to love and trust each other more. All the nations of the world are beginning to mingle with each other; why should India alone be excluded from this great family of nations, and be shut up within her own limits, within her own borders, instead of sharing with others all the advantages that different nations possess? This question of travelling is one of greater importance at the present time, than perhaps you may think. The mind is enlarged, the character grows wider and nobler by travel. How can you know the great forward movement of the world, if you are entirely shut out from it? The world is moving, whether you move or not; other nations are growing, whether you grow or not; you may turn your back on them, but they will go on growing all the same; and the danger is that they are assimilating Indian thought, they are assimilating Indian philosophy, and are beginning to share something of the spirituality of Indian religion. They are getting from you all they want, and you are getting nothing in return, because you shut yourselves in. Do you know that your ideas of the outer world are exceedingly erroneous and exceedingly mistaken? Over and over again, among educated and thoughtful men, I find most absurd ideas of foreign nations, and suspicions that have no basis in reality. We cannot have brotherhood, until we learn to know each other, and learn to love each other. And shall India be excluded from the Human Brotherhood, and be marked off by selfish isolation in the centuries to come?

No, I do not believe that this is possible. But a definite change in this respect should be made by the thoughtful, and this tyranny of outcasting for travel should be thrown off.

It is fair to say that the prejudice against foreign travel has a real foundation, in the results that it too often has upon those who go, under the present conditions. I admit, as far as the most orthodox Hindu admits, that the effect of Western travel on many young men is deplorable to the very last extent. But that is not because of the travel; it is because of the conditions with which that travel is surrounded. When your young sons go abroad, when they are thrown into foreign society, without any elders to take care of them, finding everything around them different from what they left at home, having no public opinion to control them, no family love to hold them, thrown into utterly new conditions, what wonder is it that they break down morally, that they become deteriorated, and pick up the worst, and not the best, of European civilisation? I know from experience, that these young men, coming to London, go into the very worst conditions that London has to offer for young men of gentle birth. Crowded into lodging-houses kept by people who are of fifth or sixth-rate grade in society, of the status of small shop-keepers and nothing more, they find in them all that they see of English Society and English social life. They do not mingle with the cultivated classes, they do not mingle with the better type of English men and English women. They go to London as strangers, with none to help and guide them. They are not to be blamed, but rather they are to be pitied, that they often pick up European vices and very rarely assimilate European virtues, that they come back with the manners of the stable and the kitchen. That state of things is to be corrected. If residence in Europe is to be made useful, they must not go as they go to-day. They must go into conditions carefully made for them, where the influence should be moral, where the training should be religious, and where the atmosphere should be refined, and then they will no longer come back, as too often they come back now, having lost Hindu virtues and acquired European vices. On the contrary, they will maintain their Hindu virtues and add to them useful European qualities; and thus the prejudice against travel will disappear, and you will reap its useful characteristics instead of the mischiefs that are found to-day.

There is another point, then, that I ask you carefully to consider. Will you introduce into the caste system uniformity of practice? Will you introduce the recognition of merits and demerits, instead of being swayed by prejudice and ignorance? Will you outcast for profligacy, for dishonouring the dharma of the caste? If that were done, outcasting would still have a useful part to play. Whereas, as used to-day, it is an instrument too often of social tyranny, of petty persecution and not of religion, and it does not really guard the purity of the castes. If it is seen that this change should be brought about, then practical steps should be taken to bring it about. Thoughtful, educated, and religious Hindus should mark out lines of action, and then deliberately walk along them, and stand by them, whatever it may cost. They should try to prevent outcasting for travel, and if it be done they should ignore it, and behave as if it had not occurred. The men who are leaders in such changes must themselves be models, spotless in life, and examples to others, in order that they may carry with them public opinion, in order that they may gradually restore all that is good in the system, while eliminating all that is evil. Hypocrisy, at present rampant, must be destroyed; that which we so often find—mere pretence of penance where no remorse is felt—must utterly be done away with. A man should be looked upon as an outcast, not because he travels, but because after he travels he performs a sham of a penance, time after time, as is too often done at the present day, with no intention in future to avoid the cause of the penance. [I have heard a man boast that he travels backwards and forwards constantly, and pays Rs. 5 on his return to his priest and performs Prayashchitta, and then is received without demur. Such Prayashchittas are blasphemies, and dishonour all who take part in them.]

There is one other point which I must touch upon before leaving the subject. Outside of all castes, there are thousands and millions of men and women born in India who are utterly neglected and treated with callous indifference. I know that in these Provinces, this question has not the same urgency as in the South. But a common interest should be felt in the questions affecting the South of India by the people of the North, as the Southern people should feel for the questions specially affecting the Northern. The vast mass of the neglected pariahs in the South are at once a menace and a disgrace to Hinduism throughout the whole country. It is among them that the missionaries gain most of their converts, not from the standpoint of religion, but from the standpoint of society. For so short-sighted are the Hindus there, that they will exclude from their houses pariahs even of decent life; but the same man who has thus been excluded will be received in their house when he is a convert to Christianity or to Islâm. What is the result? That Hinduism is becoming undermined, and Mahummedans and Christians are increasing in the South. In the South, you find the Christian converts are numbered by thousands and thousands, and when you ask about them you hear that they are drawn mostly from the pariahs. When they are converted, they take a social step upwards. And what wonder that they take that step, when they find no other way of inclusion in society open to them? Is it wise to undermine Hinduism in that fashion? And as this pariah population increases, and the relative proportion changes between it and the castes, we shall find Hinduism becoming weaker and weaker, and larger and larger masses of people growing up outside it, instead of within it. Would it not be wiser for the learned amongst you to devise some way in which it would be possible to reach these people, to teach them, to give them simple principles of religion and some moral and religious training, and to treat them with such respect as they can win by their character? Would it not be wiser to do this from within Hinduism, rather than multiply other religions which are inimical to Hinduism, and which undermine Hinduism, and threaten its social stability?

Such, then, are some of the problems that lie before you, problems certainly not so deep as those with which before we have been dealing in previous Conventions, but problems that are being discussed more than ever in India, and which are dividing society into those who will have no change on one side, and those who demand a total abolition of caste on the other. Here lies the peril of India—this division of her people into two opposing camps, this division into two parties—one which will not move at all, the other which wants to move away from all the old ideals, from all that has made India distinctive among the nations of the world,

I am trying to win you to a medium course, to one which shall cling to the old ideals, shall purify the modern actualities, shall re-establish the ancient religion and the ancient social system, instead of the mere burlesques of them, which is all we have in modern days. I know that these social changes are perhaps the most difficult of all, because they are so mixed up with family traditions, with social customs, with the whole fabric of ordinary daily life; yet the question is one of life or death, one of progress or extinction. It is because of that, that I have used such plain words in speaking to you of it, and that I have described some of the scandals and the evils that we see around us.

You know well enough, that all through India, I have spoken in favour of the ancient system, the essential system of the four great castes, that I hold the restoration of that system to be vital to the welfare of India, that I believe it to be the best system that was ever organised, that the evolution of the soul can go on within it better than in any other. Just because I hold it so valuable, just because I believe it to be so vital, I desire to preserve it in India. But I tell you it cannot be preserved much longer under the present conditions, and that it is already tottering to its fall, owing to the justifiable attacks that are assailing it from all sides. Among the educated classes, it is becoming more and more disapproved; continually among thoughtful men we find a growing rebellion, a growing revolt against that which cannot be justified either by religion or by reason. And just because it is valuable, let us try to preserve it; do not let abuses destroy it, do not let the most ignorant be the most powerful and rule the caste. Let the educated take the question into their own hands; let the learned decide, and not the ignorant multitude; it is for the learned to lead, and it is for the ignorant to follow. Wisdom is the only true basis of authority. By right thinking and right reason must the Caste System be reformed, if it is to be reformed at all. [The educated and pure living members of a caste are seriously in fault when they stand idly aside and allow the authority of their caste to be wielded unfairly, cruelly, and inappropriately. Here, as in so many cases, the lethargy and want of public spirit of the educated Indian are to blame.]

Inasmuch as it is interwoven with the very life of India, inasmuch as Hinduism without caste is practically unthinkable, I ask you, I plead with you, that you will not let prejudice stand in the way, nor let tradition blind you to the necessity of the times; discuss the question earnestly, seriously, without passion, without antagonism, and in your wisdom devise some remedy for the evils, so that we may again feel, with the great Author of the system, that it emanates from Him; then will the system flourish as it was intended to do, and again the four-fold order may regenerate the future India.

LECTURE IV.

WOMANHOOD.

MY BROTHERS:—

It has been said that the position of woman in any civilisation shows the stage of evolution at which that civilisation has arrived; and if that maxim be taken as accurate, then there can be no kind of doubt as to the height of civilisation attained in ancient India, when we contemplate the position which there was held by women, and study the types that then were found in the land. You may search the history of the world, you may turn over the pages of the world's literature; nowhere will you find stronger, sweeter, and more beautiful types of womanhood than you find in the ancient literature of India. It seems as if every ideal virtue, as if every possible grace, had been gathered together, had been welded into human forms, and then those forms set on high to attract the admiration of the world. The names of some of those great women are "familiar as household words" both in the East and in the West. Western writers, western thinkers, western philosophers, have not been slow to recognise their ideal beauty, and to point to them as showing out the perfection of womanhood, as giving to the world types which have never been excelled. I might quote to you passage after passage from western writers, showing you the impression made upon the mind of the West by these sublime types of womanhood. I want to lay stress upon them in the beginning of this discourse; because here, as elsewhere, I look to ancient India for the model and ideal, in order to give reason and inspiration why modern India should change her ways in some very definite respects. Only as we realise the greatness of the past, only as we contrast it with the poverty of the present, can we see clearly the road along which we should direct our steps, if we desire to bring back in modern days the glory of those ancient times. For, as I told you in the beginning, in regard to these important questions of the day, there is a party that desires to change everything, and a party that desires to change nothing, and between these two unpractical schools, the future destiny of India is swinging to-day. How shall we know what reforms to choose and what to reject, unless we are familiar with the ancient ideals, unless we are able, by studying them, to recognise the goal to which our steps are to be directed? Only as these inspire us, can changes be wisely chosen, and steadily carried out. Only as these draw our hearts by their beauty, shall we be able to raise our mother India to the position that she should occupy amid the nations of the world.

In studying ancient India, there are certain points about the womanhood of that time that come out very clearly and distinctly: the theory of womanhood, that which you may call the philosophical view; the place that woman occupies in Nature; the functions that are especially woman's to discharge; the great division of sexes that we find in humanity, nay, in all Nature, a distinction certainly not without the profoundest meaning, certainly not without its great significance in evolution. Any attempt to bridge over that difference, any attempt to turn a man into a woman, or a woman into a man, means the throwing back of humanity, a check on its orderly, on its progressive evolution. Certain distinct qualities are evolved in each sex; certain distinct powers are found assigned to the one sex or to the other. To try to unsex either, is to make a fundamental blunder; and we need to have our theory clear and distinct, ere our practices can be wisely and rightly directed.

What, then, is the ancient Hindu theory as regards the nature and function of womanhood? We are told at the very beginning of creative work, when humanity was to be produced, the Creator divided himself into two halves, one half male and the other female. This division of the Divine into two, marks, as it were, the very basis of our theory. Both sexes are equally Divine, each is one half of God; both sexes have their part to play in human evolution, and in the evolution of the world as a whole. The sex distinction is not simply found in humanity, it goes through all the kingdoms of Nature, even though the name of sex is not universally applied. The two great sides of the manifested God in Nature are found in the sexes; on one side show the different attributes and functions which in humanity are found in the male, and on the other side the attributes and functions which in humanity are found in the female. So also we know that in the whole theory of the Devas, you do not find a Deva without a Devî. These two are inseparable, indivisible: the dual manifestation of one life, of one Being.

[The difference of the qualities evolved renders it impossible to develop both sets simultaneously in the same physical form; hence two series of forms, in which the predominant physical characteristics differ; in one of these series the intellectual qualities find their best expression, in the other the emotional. These forms are the male and female, and their value to evolution lies in their difference. As evolution nears its ending, the differences become less marked, until the two are united, the halves of one body as at first.]

Half of the Divine nature, then, comes forth in womanhood; that side of the Divine nature which is connected with the making of forms, which gives the soil in which forms are developed, which nourishes them, guards them, protects them; in a word, the Mother-side of Nature. That is the fundamental distinction, then, that we find in the ancient writings, that the woman represents the material side of the manifested universe, which is necessary for the manifestation of spirit—the Mother-side of Nature, that nutritive, protective side. This is the fundamental type of womanhood, and marks out woman's functions in the universe.

So as we study further the ancient teachings, we notice that wherever divine power is to be manifested, wherever there is a need for the exertion of Divine energy, there the female Divine manifestation is called forth, appears, and executes that which needs to be done. If you turn to the well-known story of the coming forth of Durgâ, what do you find? You find that the world was terribly oppressed by the Asuras, and that the Devas did not know how to protect themselves. You find them going to the great Gods for help, appealing to those Divine powers for protection. And then, as the story unfolds, you find that out of the Gods Themselves there comes forth the mighty radiant form of Durgâ; that in Her the Divine forces were embodied. It was Durgâ who, by those forces and energies, delivered the world from the terror under which it was panic-stricken. It was that mighty Durgâ who swept out of the path of the Gods the terrible antagonists who then were barring the way. Thus is shown out the idea for all times, that in the Divine Woman, the Goddess-side of Nature, all power is manifested, all protection is to be sought. There is the remover of obstacles, there the one who lifts us over dangers. The Divine Womanhood is the refuge of the world, and at the feet of the Goddess all the worlds find rest.

Such is the thought, then, which continually

comes out in Hindu teachings, as underlying the Hindu idea of Womanhood.

When we pass on still further to see how in the human being this is manifested, we find the ideal of marriage held up as constituting the complete true human being. Husband and wife are not thought of as two, but they are thought of as one. Husband and wife are not thought of as separate, they are thought of as united. Husband and wife are not thought of as capable of division, they are but two halves constituting an entire, a single whole. Just as in the Deva and Devî one Divine life is manifested, so in the husband and wife the perfect type of humanity is shown forth. There is no idea of possible antagonism. There is no idea of possible rivalry. Man and woman, husband and wife, are two halves of the complete Man, of the complete Human Life—that perfect Union, that true Unity, gave the Hindu Ideal of Marriage.

Then we study the very form and physical constitution of woman, we find that this, her function in Nature, is marked on her very body, as well as her inner nature. We find that the whole body of the ideal woman is formed to typify, to express, to show forth, all the grace and strength of emotion, all the profundity and height of love. The woman typifies, in the perfect human being, the side of emotion, just as the man typifies, in that same human being, the type of intellect. Both are equally necessary, both form parts of the perfect whole, and both are constituted in their several physical composition for the showing forth of these two characteristic marks of humanity. When the two are united, when the intellect gives the directing force, and the emotion gives the impulsive force, then only is right action possible, then only can humanity fulfil its function in the world. The two thus blended together, the two thus working as a perfect whole, give us the ideal human type towards which humanity is approaching. Anything that destroys that unity, anything that separates one sex from the other in life or interest, anything that tends to draw them apart, to bring them into competition, to set them in rivalry the one against the other, anything of that kind is fatal to the progress of the race, and is turning evolution along the road that tends downwards and not upwards.

This fundamental, this true, theory is one which has to be grasped, which has to be clung to, through the whole of our study of the subject. In woman you will find the emotions most strongly shown, most fully developed; she suffers more keenly, she enjoys more keenly, than man either suffers or enjoys. Therefore, in dealing with her, when we come to consider the question of education, we have to take care to the utmost to draw out her especial capacity, but also, and this is vital, to take care that it is not developed without also developing in her the other, though the subordinate, side of her nature, the intellectual. Just as in man you have to prevent him from becoming hard and selfish, by training and developing his emotional and moral nature, so in woman it is also necessary to train and develop the side of intelligence, else she will be unregulated and unbalanced. For though in man the intellect should dominate emotion, yet both are necessary for an all-round character; and though in woman emotion should be more highly developed than intellect, yet both should also be found in her. Then when man and woman thus developed are joined together there is a perfect marriage, both are able to work together and to understand each other, to be true companions, friends, and helpmates along the path of life. Whereas the exaggerated development of the specific side of either, and the non-development of the secondary side, makes a perfect union of lives impossible; they are too far apart, have too little common ground, and there is therefore always the likelihood of jarring and disagreement, making the marriage less perfect than it ought to be, making the note that is struck less rich and less harmonious than it should be.

When we come to look at the ideal of marriage union as shown forth in Hindu literature what do we find? We find most perfect, most unbounded love, the deepest reverence, as parts of the character of the ideal wife; a fidelity that knows no possibility of change, a courage that can hold to the one against every opposing circumstance, a love that does not falter even under the uttermost strain, a strength that never wavers, no matter how great the difficulty, how sore the trial. Then on the side of the husband, we find unfailing tenderness, continual protection, power and will to guide, unfaltering love; so that in this union all the noblest relations of humanity are gathered up, and the ideal Hindu husband and the ideal Hindu wife make the most perfect picture of the marriage union that has ever served as ideal of a nation, that has ever inspired practice in right living.

And when from that theory, we turn to the practice in ancient India, what there do we find? The study of the ancient books shows us that woman in ancient India shines out strongly in practice, shows the characteristics of the ideal woman, in all the functions, in all the duties of life. The law is laid down as to her position in the famous shlokas of Manu, where it is declared that:—

"Women are to be honoured and adorned by fathers and brothers, by husbands, as also by brothers-in-law, who desire much prosperity.

"Where women are honoured, there the Gods rejoice; but where they are not honoured, there all rites are fruitless.

"Where women grieve, that family quickly perishes; but where they do not grieve, that (family) ever prospers.

"Houses which women, not honoured, curse, those, as if blighted by magic, perish utterly." (Manu, III., 55, 56, 57, 58.)

Passing from these precepts, which embody the theory, to the practice whereof I spoke, I want to put before you certain definite facts as regards the life of woman in ancient India. The first point is as to the position of women in ancient India, in the home and outside the home, the latter a type of women who have almost entirely disappeared from modern India. You find in ancient India that there existed a class of women who did not enter into the marriage relation. They were called by the specific name of Brahmavâdinîs, teachers of the Veda. Their position was recognised, clear, and distinct. They are spoken of in the ancient Law books. The special privileges that they enjoyed are clearly laid down in the Shâstras. We are told that women were divided into two classes, Brahmavâdinîs and the married. The first class wore the sacred thread, had the right of kindling the sacrificial fire, studied and taught the Vedas, and lived unmarried in their own houses. I am quoting, as regards their rights and privileges, from the writings of Harita as translated. Other authorities might be quoted on the same lines. There were female ascetics as well as male ascetics; you will remember, for instance, the one who came into the court of King Janaka, carrying the daṇḍa, wearing the ascetic robes, going her way as a teacher, appearing in the very court of the king to carry on discussion on subtle points of religion and philosophy. This class of women in ancient India, these knowers of the Supreme, show clearly and definitely that women in those ancient days were not excluded from the knowledge of the Vedas, were not excluded from taking part in the great discussions upon philosophy and religion, proving that the precepts against a woman studying, or even hearing, the

Vedas must be interpolations of a later date. They were learned as men were learned, and they even taught the Vedas as men were teachers. Some of the Mantras of the Vedas, some of the hymns of the *Rig Veda*, were originally given through women; through their mouths the sacred Mantras were spoken, which in these modern days their daughters may not study nor repeat. Not only is it true that some of the Rig verses were given by women, but we also find their names in the list of spiritual teachers, in the list of great Áchâryas, who form the chain of spiritual teachers. I need hardly remind you that in the Upaṇiṣhads you read of such a knower of Brahman as Gârgî, who questioned Yâgnyavalkya in the great assembly of sages, being given her place there to put questions as she would.

Even without looking on that special class, even without taking those noble types of Virgin Womanhood, we find that the women of the household—the wives and mothers—also enjoyed a large amount of liberty and took their part in a number of public ceremonies. Some of the hymns of the *Rig Veda* indeed, just mentioned, were written by wives. We also find records in the *Rig Veda* itself of great festivals attended by women who were wives and mothers. We find in the *Râmâyana*, that Kaushalyâ, the mother of Râma Chandra, was actually the officiating priestess at a great sacrifice at which were gathered vast crowds of kings, of nobles, of Brâhmaṇas, and of the people at large. She performed the act of sacrifice, hers was the hand of the officiator. We find they took part in the discussions that occurred between their husbands and sages, as in the cases of Draupadî and Sîtâ. We find them advising and counselling their husbands in matters of difficulty, in matters concerning the outer world. Both Sîtâ and Draupadî showed knowledge of the world, understood the ways in which things went on in the external world, were able to give wise counsel to their husbands, to estimate the forces of opposing opinions, and to exercise judgment as to the path which it was best to follow. You find a woman called into a great assembly to give counsel when Duryodhana had set himself against Shrî Kriṣhṇa, and his father, his preceptor, and his elders had all striven in vain to turn him from his purpose; as the last resort, his mother, Gândhârî, was sent for; she came into that great asemblage, and there addressed her son in words of remonstrance, reproof, and counsel, showing how in those days women were really wise and great, that their counsel was highly valued, that their advice was respectfully listened to and followed, because knowledge gave them the power to speak, and learning and wisdom gave them the authority to pronounce their opinion.

Studying these cases, which can be multiplied a hundredfold, we come to a very definite opinion with regard to the position of women in ancient India, and we see that they enjoyed a wide and deep education and a dignified liberty. While the marriage relation was close and indivisible, while the husband was regarded as the head, as the Lord and as the Guru, nay, even as representing God Himself, while there was that complete unity, which we find in India alone, and a complete subordination of the wife to the husband, yet this did not prevent woman from exercising lofty functions, from playing her part in the family and in the world, and so in making up that perfect human judgment and action which only come where both sexes are joined together, and where the wisdom of each conduces to right judgment and to right activity. That is but a poor imperfect picture of the part that women played in those ancient days. Clearly here we have the signs of high intelligence; clearly here we have the signs of deep and wide education of women in ancient days; we have here nobly developed types of womanhood, women of heroic stature, women of grand and inspiring power. No wonder that Indian marriage has won the admiration of the world, when such types of womanhood and wifehood are found scattered throughout the records of ancient literature, and when all this greatness and nobility form an integral part of the woman's life.

When we contrast with this the position of women in modern India, how great, how saddening, is the change. Woman still keeps her exquisite spirituality, she still shows forth her strong and perfect devotion. Looking over all the types of women that the modern world presents, travelling as I have done in country after country, and coming into contact with all the different types of womanhood, evolved under different civilisations, I bear you witness that I have found nowhere spirituality so pure and lofty, devotion so strong and tender, purity so unsullied and spotless, patience so wise and beautiful, as are found even in the modern women of India.

Undeveloped and restricted as are now their lives, yet they present a most gracious type, and when sometimes I have been thinking of one or another whom I have met, sometimes when I have been studying the beauty of character of the type

—of the unique type of Indian womanhood—I have thought what India might be if all the possibilities in India's women had an opportunity of flowing out and actually coming into manifestation. When I have seen what they are under circumstances so disadvantageous, when I have seen what still they are, despite the narrow environment into which they are penned, I have thought that it may be that India's redemption may still be brought about by India's women; for when once the woman's heart is touched, she is a thousand times more devoted than are men. She is willing to sacrifice herself as a man will never sacrifice himself. Through thousands of years, through thousands of generations, women have learned the lesson of self-sacrifice, in the home, with the husband, with the child; and when that spirit of self-sacrifice, now instinctive, a part of her spiritual nature, is turned to the highest object, is directed to the noblest ends, there is then a power for good that nothing else can give to the world. In the self-sacrifice and devotion of her women, it may be that India's redemption will find its real instrument.

But in order that it may be so, some of the conditions under which women are growing up must be changed. And this change is necessitated largely by the changes which are passing over the whole of India at the present time—by the pressure of Western education on the fathers and husbands, on the brothers and sons. These changes in the men necessitate certain changes in the women also, else too wide a gulf is made between man and woman, their lives grow utterly apart, are carried on along too much separated lines The woman, not knowing of the larger interests of the man's life, is not capable of the wise counsel that in older days she was ever ready to give to husband and son. Shut out as she is to-day, but as she was not in the past, from the reasonable enjoyment of and participation in the world around her, you find her growing narrower in mind, whilst still she keeps her purity in heart. We have to deal with that modern innovation, in order to prevent the evil results growing out therefrom.

Now, we all know that some of the conditions that are to be eliminated have rather been imposed from without, than evolved from within. The conditions under which large parts of the country have had to live, the Mussulmân invasion, the lack of safety of life and honour, dearer still than life—these are the causes which have brought about the system of seclusion, which is not Áryan. The Zenâna is not a Hindu custom, but preeminently a Mussulmân custom. The system of Zenâna does not belong to ancient India. All the literature of ancient India gives proofs to the contrary on that point. It has grown out of danger, in times when it became absolutely necessary to put a wall of that sort round womanhood, in order to preserve her from perils which it would have been impossible for her to face. It is not a matter for blame, it is only a matter for regret, that those conditions became necessary in some parts of the country. In parts of the country where there has not been Mussulmân dominion, the Hindu women have kept a large part of the ancient self-respect, dignity, and liberty, and are not under the very narrow seclusion system which is the characteristic of those parts of the country where the Mussulmân has ruled for long. That is a point to bear in mind very clearly. For if it were possible, however slowly and however gradually, to enlarge these restrictive limits, to gradually widen out the life of the woman, you would not be following the West, but following your own ancestral custom; you would only be giving back to the modern women what the ancient Indian women continually enjoyed.

Of course, the greatest difficulty of any change in this respect will come from the women themselves, and not from the men. I know that, in many cases, husbands and fathers would be very glad to widen out the restrictions, but the opposition comes from those who have grown up in them, who for generations have been trained on these lines. The only way of bringing about a gradual change, which will not do more harm than good, is to educate, educate, educate, and so slowly and gradually evolve the intelligence of women, bringing them back to the high level which once they occupied here.

Let me point out to you that the present condition of women in India, as regards education, is far worse than it was even two or three generations ago. We know that the elder women are better educated than the younger generation. The younger generation has fallen, as it were, between two stools. The old education is no longer imparted; the modern education does not take its place.

With regard to that modern education, permit me to say that you will be most unwise, if you adopt for the education of your women, a mere copy of the education given to Western women. That is not the kind of education that you need. It would not build up women of the ancient Áryan type. Think for a moment what female education is meant to do in the West. Owing to the social conditions there, a very large number of women remain unmarried. There is an enormous class of unmarried women there, who practically have no supporters. They are not supported as to their ordinary livelihood by fathers, who pass away, by brothers who have their own households to look after, and they are left to support themselves and to gain their own livelihood. Now, that gaining of their livelihood leads them necessarily into competition with men. They enter the labour market, and they have to follow the trading conditions in regard to the various means of gaining a livelihood. Out of that competition, out of that struggle for existence, out of that passing of women into the public arena of life-struggle, where they have to gain their own livelihood and fight for their own hands against the competition of men, out of that has arisen the demand for what is called the higher education of women. Its object is that the women, educated on the same lines as men, may be able to compete with them in the various walks of life, and earn their own livelihood, as men earn theirs. That is the economic reason underlying the demand for higher education. I presume that no Hindu, unless he has lost the Hindu heart, desires to bring about that economic condition of things here. I presume that he does not desire to educate his daughters, and then to send them out into the world to struggle with men for gaining a livelihood, to compete with men in the various learned professions, in the various commercial undertakings. Truly, no Hindu can desire to bring about such a regrettable stage of social evolution. But if not, why adopt a type of education designed for such a stage? It is undesirable that Indian girls should be trained along those unsuitable lines. What you want to do is to devise a system of education which shall make them ideal Indian women of ancient types, fitting them, for the most part, for the life of wives and mothers, and, in rare cases, for that knowledge of Brahman which may make them, under these conditions as it did under the older conditions, the spiritual teachers and helpers of humanity.

But for that, what ought to be the education? First, it is clear that the elements of the ordinary vernacular education must be given to them, with a knowledge of Saṁskrit and its literature, so that they may be able to read of the great ideals of Womanhood and desire to reproduce those in their own lives. This should be the foundation of woman's education: a knowledge of the vernacular, from the literary standpoint; and a knowledge of the mother language Saṁskrit, in which is stored up the sacred literature of India. It would be wise, though many of you will probably disagree with that, as a novel idea, if you introduced also the knowledge of the English tongue. By doing that, you would bring them into touch with the lines of thought along which their husbands and their sons are travelling, and would thus enable them to appreciate the tendencies and influences which are playing upon the men, and to neutralise some of the evils which arise from those influences when left unchecked. At the present time, men are too much inclined to go along sceptical and materialistic lines, because of the education they receive. Women, utterly shut out of all knowledge, cannot mentally meet them anywhere, and appeal to them by that which has influence over them. Shut up into a narrow, lonely, unthinking life, left often superstitious rather than enlightened in their faith, they fail to influence men, for the man puts aside the opinion of women, generally thinking that it is not worthy of consideration because of their lack of education. With extreme care, then, so that you may not injure the type of womanhood, as the type of manhood has been injured, you might introduce the nobler, purer side of European thought, and bring that within the reach of the women of India. Then they would know something of modern life, and they would be able to appreciate better the conditions amidst which their husbands have to live and work. They would again become counsellors at home, as they cannot be now that they are utterly excluded from all knowledge of the outer world. Now-a-days, from ignorance of outside conditions, they continually press for things that are impossible, and often make difficulties where none should exist, in regard to the training and instruction of the young.

Then you should add to that education, an education scientific in its character, along the lines which should make the women more useful as the queens of the home. She should be taught in modern India, as she was taught in ancient India, the elements of hygiene, physiology, and nutrition, so that she may guide the household wisely and well, so that you may not have to call in a doctor for every trivial ailment and difficulty. The older women still are wiser than many of the younger generation, who are ignorant, and therefore useless. In tracing out education for the women, this ancient element ought again to be included, so that you may build up a wise, patient, religious, clear-judging woman, who shall be her husband's friend, counsellor, and helper, as well as the joy of his heart, and the delight of his life.

It might be well, in addition, if you added to that literary, scientific, and religious education, some elements also of artistic training. How much might be added to the happiness and brightness of the home, if the girls of the home were trained, to some extent, along artistic lines? I know how much prejudice there is in India against artistic training, especially where music is concerned, because of the shameful associations that have grown up in connection with vocal and instrumental music. But those do not belong to the Art itself; they are part of the degradation of modern India, of the degradation of Indian men and women. Your sons, if they would have music, must go into bad and degraded conditions. If they would have emotional delight, and all young men crave it, they cannot have it at home; and so they go for it amid the lowest of the population, and mix with the most shameful of companions. Is that wise? Is that right? So strongly is this felt, that in some parts of India, men of high and respectable families have started classes, where girls of similar families may be trained in instrumental and vocal music. Although at first the movement met with very great opposition, although at first harsh and cruel things were said about those who led it, yet gradually it is making its way; and girls thus taught—I was told in Madras by the very Brâhmaṇa who was instructing them—those girls are most eagerly sought in marriage, because of this accomplishment, which has made them a bright adornment of the home. More and more in Madras, this kind of education is spreading, and is breaking down prejudice, and is making the homes brighter for the young, more attractive especially to the Western-educated boys.

Along these lines, then, I would suggest that education should go, and not along the lines along which, to a very small extent, it is now-a-days carried out in India.

But I should not be dealing fairly with you, if I did not say that there is one tremendous obstacle in the way of this—an obstacle which I know not if you will be strong enough and wise enough to surmount—that is, that such an education cannot be given, if child-motherhood is to remain a part of Indian life. If the girl-child is to be made a mother, then she can never grow to the real height of motherhood; so that here again the question turns on this same pivot of early marriage that I spoke of in the first lecture, and will have to be decided by your own thoughtful and deliberate consideration.

There are two ways in which a woman may be treated—one the ancient way, one the modern way; one, I venture to say, a natural and so a wise way, the other an artificial and so a foolish way; one that makes for construction, and the other that makes for gradual destruction. The ancient and wise way was training, educating, raising the woman, putting her more and more on a high level, and then giving her a reasonable and dignified liberty. The modern and foolish way is keeping her ignorant and undeveloped, childish and irrational, and then shutting her in within a narrow environment. There are few things more beautiful in life than the way in which the Indian son loves, reverences, and obeys his mother. But if that most beautiful of relations is to continue under the modern conditions for boys in India, you will have to meet their needs by educating the women who are their mothers. You all know the obedience that the Indian son shows to the mother, how he treats her practically as a Goddess, whose words must not be challenged, whose lightest wish must be utterly and completely obeyed. If that exquisite relation is to preserve its life under the changed conditions, you will have to get rid of the narrowness that too often marks the woman's opinion at present, because of her utter shutting out from the external world, her shutting into the in-door life. If you would preserve that—and to lose it would be the saddest of losses, one that India would scarcely survive—you must gradually raise the womanhood of India, so that the mother's words may be wise as well as loving, may be broad instead of narrow, may meet the conditions of the day instead of entirely ignoring them, may not make unreasonable demands, demands which are sometimes felt to be unreasonable, even while the man yields himself to them from the instinct of love and obedience. This is a necessary condition for preserving that exquisite relationship, one that the men must take into their hands; for all the power is lodged in their hands. While a woman is very very young and very fair, unreasonableness may seem almost an added charm in the eyes of some; the petulance of a graceful child is felt as amusing and pretty; but when the child has grown to a woman of mature years, that lack of judging impartially and reasonably is felt as a difficulty, is felt as a hindrance, is felt as a disadvantage and annoyance. In order that the woman's influence may be preserved; in order that she may not lose her hold over the respect as well as the hearts of her husband and her sons: in order that she may really be one half of humanity, as she ought to be; in order that she may play her part well in the home, may train up her sons as they ought to be trained; in order that she may exercise an elevating power over the children round her knees, may prove a worthy mother to worthy sons; this question must be considered and dealt with by the wise amongst you; else the gulf between Western-trained men and uneducated women will widen, despite all love, despite all tenderness, despite all longing to remain together. For the influences are mighty which are tending to divide, and unless those influences are checked, that old great Ideal of marriage will disappear and be seen no more.

This, then, is the line of thought that I would suggest to you with regard to the Womanhood of India: that you should study and realise the old Ideal, and that you should then see how it may be re-introduced; that you should educate women everywhere, and choose wisely the kind of education that you give; that you should keep in mind the capacities that they have, that you should evolve those to the utmost of your ability; so that in the future, as in the past, there may be great, heroic, strong, pure, and devoted women in India;

for sooner or later, weakness means degradation; sooner or later, the lack of strength leads to lack of love and lack of fidelity.

My Brothers, I have gone over in these lectures many difficult problems, many thorny questions, on which inevitably much difference of opinion must arise. The slow deterioration of centuries, of thousands of years, cannot be undone in a moment, cannot be changed by a single effort; nay, the very need of changing is not seen by very many of you, so thoroughly are you the men of your own times—the result of this long course of change. The more the ancient Ideals can be studied, the more will these modern spectacles drop from your eyes, and you will see the need for change, you will see the necessity for exertion. It is to the elders I appeal, for in your hands is the power, and in your hands *ought* to be the power and in the hands of none other. On this point, I do not appeal to the young, to the growing lads. It is not for them to deal with these questions, it is not for them to initiate reforms. If you leave it to them, the reforms will be hasty, ill-considered, headlong, with all the natural impulsive hasty judgment of youth. It is to you, the fathers, mature men, men of middle age, it is for you to consider these questions, and to look into the immediate future. You are responsible for sending your boys to an education which is changing their views of life. You are responsible for sending them to Missionary Schools or to Government Schools and Colleges, where their faith is undermined, where the old Ideals are destroyed, where the new thoughts are poured into them, without any restriction or limitation; then, looking at the results, you are inclined to complain. Large numbers of them are thoroughly Westernised; large numbers care nothing for the old Ideals; large numbers are bent upon reproducing the social and economic conditions of the West, of which they know so little, of which they dream and imagine so much.

What will be the result? You are going to pass away from India, and are leaving the future in these young hands. You cannot long stand where you are standing to-day, you cannot stand there for ever; you will have to leave your places for that where the fire will receive you, and whence your ashes will be cast into Gangâ. Then these young men will make the India of the future, and mould that India as they will. Therefore it is to you I plead. If you will deal with them aright, if you will put before them in your own lives the old Ideals, that they may imitate them; if at all times you will recognise what there is of justice in their longings, and feel sympathy with their aspirations; if you will not turn a deaf ear to everything that they say; if, when they want to go forward, you will share to some extent in their hopes, and guide them, and not turn a deaf ear to all they plead for; then you may direct and mould them, and so turn the future of India into the right path. If you will not, then you are digging the grave of India, and she will go down into that grave after you have passed away.

It is all very well to say that all social reform is bad. I grant that much of the spirit in which it is now carried on is bad and mischievous. It is foolish that the old Ideals should be utterly disregarded, and it is true that the acceptance of many of these reforms, in the spirit in which they are made, would be the ruin of India as a people, would be the destruction of her religion as a living force. I grant all that. But I tell you that there is equal danger on the other side. Dogged conservatism, fossilised orthodoxy which will not move, men who will only stand fixed in their conceit where they are, while all around them is moving, men who will not consider the moving wheels of time—those men are as dangerous to India's religious future, as those who will utterly Westernise her, and so wipe her out from among the nations. It is because of that, that I have spoken upon these subjects to-day, in what is the most conservative city in the whole of India. It is because of this danger to India that lies in the future, this growing up of the young generation under the glamour of Western civilisation, Western thought, apart from all Hindu traditions, that I have spoken to-day. Unless you can win it to the old Ideals, and penetrate it with the spirit of the ancient faith, there is no hope for the future of India.

There is what you really need.' There is the path that wisdom points out for your treading. Be willing to get rid of your bias, be willing to introduce reforms, and change the customs which are harmful and mischievous. Do not be frightened away from change by the red rag of "social reform"; do not be deceived into the idea that because one kind is bad, therefore all change is dangerous. You must admit that India is not what she ought to be. You must admit that there are abuses on every side. You must know that a distinctly large number of educated youths are becoming more and more alienated from the ancient modes of life. It is no good to blame them: it is no good to denounce them. You should try to win them, try to induce them to follow the wiser path. Show sympathy and not antagonism, and so you gain influence over their hearts and their lives. Is India to be split up into two parts, one which will change nothing, and the other which will change all? If that be the future that you deliberately choose, then indeed the destiny of India is fixed and will not alter; then her place will go to another nation; her function of teaching will pass to another people. Stones that will not move are left behind by the current; and if the current be not wisely directed, but a dam be built across it, then after a while, when the current gets enough strength, the dam is swept away and the waters flood the country, and destroy instead of fertilising. It is that great danger which the educational movement started by us in this Central Hindu College is intended to ward off. It is intended to weld together the old Ideals and the modern spirit; that is what we are doing in this place; it is that road along which lies India's salvation. While we are dealing with the young, it would not be wise to leave out of account the mature. While we are trying to educate the future, the present should be modified as the field wherein that future must express itself.

My last words to you, my Brothers, are words of appeal, not to let prejudice blind you, not to let custom be an obstacle in the way. Let not the conservative instinct of the ancient civilisation make you utterly close your eyes to the needs of the present, to the demands of the future. I make my appeal to you, because I love ancient India so well, because I still nurse within my heart the hope of India's resurrection. As she is lying to-day, she is prone on the ground, helpless, degraded, without power, with only the forms, the shells of the ancient, the mighty religion that was once her glory; nothing scarcely of its power, and little of its knowledge remain. Strangled in the fetters of customs that have grown around her limbs through centuries and millenniums, bound by these iron fetters so that she can scarcely move either hands or feet—is she to lie there till her swoon passes into death, so that the only light that India shall again give to the world shall be the light of her funeral pyre, the flames in which is perishing a dead civilisation? Some say that is inevitable; some declare that there is no hope of her resurrection; that the life has gone from her, and will pass into one or other of the nations of the world. I cannot believe it, I will not accept it, until all forces to rouse her have proved fruitless, until all struggles cease, and no sign of life is seen. If there be but a few hundred hearts among India's children, who love their country better than they love themselves; if there be here and there hearts that can be set on fire with enthusiasm, with devotion, clean and strong hearts that can place themselves on the altar as an offering to the High Gods that India may live, although some of her sons may perish; if India has still in her something of her ancient spirit of love, of patriotism, and of devotion, then it is possible that the change we long for may come, and India, re-born into the modern world, may be greater than ever she was in her glorious past. I believe that still the choice lies before her: still there are two paths before her—one leading upwards, and the other downwards; one rising gradually up till she shall stand again on the pinnacle of the spiritual teacher of mankind, the other sinking slowly downwards through the throes of dying agony to the place where she shall perish, and only her ashes shall remain.

Choose *you*—the choice is yours and not mine. One human tongue can do but little, one human heart has but little force in it; it may break, but it cannot make a nation, if the nation will not make itself. I can but speak to you; I cannot do your work. I can bring to you the message of truth; I cannot make you accept it. Yours is the responsibility, not mine; yours the choice, not mine. I have done my duty when I have spoken, and pointed out to you the path which will lead to the redemption of India. If you see that path to be right, but shrink from taking it because of the difficulties and the oppositions that cumber it, then indeed you are not worthy to tread it, for it is a path for heroes and not for feeble souls. Choose you your answer, for it is an answer alike to Karma, to the world, and to the Gods, and take the responsibility which is on you, and act as you will. For me, so long as breath remains in me, I shall strive to help this land, the greatest of all lands in the past, the greatest of all lands in the future, if you will. Those who will work, let them come and work; those who will sleep, let them sleep until their country dies. Then, in far other births and other lands, you may look backwards with sorrow and regret to what India once was, but what again she shall never be. For the choice that the Gods give is a choice that, once made, is endless in its results. Choose you, then, what you will, and may the High Gods inspire you to choose aright.

AFTERWORD.

The suggestions put forward in these lectures are meant to be lived, not merely read, and that by men who love Hinduism, who are religious as well as moral. They may be summed up under the following heads:

1.—A resolve not to marry their sons before 18, nor to allow the marriage to be consummated before 20; the first marriage (betrothal) of their daughters to be thrown as late as possible, from 11 to 14, and the second (consummation) from 14 to 16.

2.—To promote the maintenance of caste relations with those who have travelled abroad, providing they conform to Hindu ways of living.

3.—To promote intermarriage and interdining between the sub-divisions of the four castes.

4.—Not to employ in any ceremony (where choice is possible) an illiterate or immoral Brahmaṇa.

5.—To educate their daughters and to promote the education of the women of their families.

6.—Not to demand any money consideration for the marriage of their children.

If pious men in all parts of India carried out these reforms individually, a vast change would be made without disturbance or excitement, but they would need to be men of clear heads and strong hearts, to meet and conquer the inevitable opposition from the ignorant and the bigoted. The worst customs that prevail are comparatively modern, but they are regarded as marks of orthodoxy and so are difficult to put aside.

I need scarcely add that I should be very happy to hear from any reader who agrees with some or all the suggestions made, or who has thoughtful criticism to offer. For only by the efforts of brave and true men can the great work outlined be accomplished.

PEACE TO ALL BEINGS.

